Praise for The Greatest Wo

"Eclectic and unique, the stories in *The Greatest Words You've Never Heard* by Steven Kayser will engage your heart and inspire your soul."

Ken Blanchard, coauthor of *The One Minute Manager*® and *Legendary Service*

"True stories of heroism, hope and heart that salute the brave victorious souls that choose to create and live lives of *significance* and *meaning*—even if they die trying. When faced with difficult times and life-defining decisions these stories can offer solace and strength, wisdom and guidance. But more importantly, they will shake your perception of reality and offer a personal challenge that will change your life ... but you won't realize that until the very last page."

Steven Pressfield, bestselling author of *Gates of Fire and The Lion's Gate*

"Wow, what a raw, powerful book. Thank you, Steve, for having the courage to show us that we serve when we dare to share challenging, heart-wrenching experiences. Anyone going through a dark night of the soul will find this book inspiring."

Ms. Sam Horn, author of *POP!* and *Tongue Fu!*

"A gifted storyteller, Steve Kayser has written a book that will touch your heart and compel you to reflect deeply on your own faith, courage, and most importantly, relationships. I couldn't put it down."

Lt. Col. Rob "Waldo" Waldman, author of the New York Times and Wall Street Journal bestseller *Never Fly Solo*

"These stories will touch your heart, but the mystery is, why haven't you read them before? Steve Kayser deserves the highest praise for digging them up."

Al Ries, author, *War in the Boardroom*

"As long as I've known Steve Kayser, he's been a connoisseur of culture and a gatherer of greatness, which he eagerly shares with everyone. Now he's produced cultural greatness himself with this book. He digs deep and harvests diamonds. Where else would you learn that while people loved Cicero's words, it was Demosthenes' powerful speech that compelled them to march? Here's your chance— dive in and be inspired!"

Skip Press, author of *How to Write What You Want and Sell What You Write* **and** *The Idiot's Guide to Screen*writing

"Steve Kayser hit a homerun with these remarkable stories that run the gamut of human experience. Each one has something powerful to tell us; Steve finds those inspirations and shares them with his characteristic sensitivity and poetic style. This book is a "must have" for your library of meaningful works!"

Marsha Friedman, CEO of EMSI Public Relations and author of *Celebritize Yourself: The Three Step Method to Increase Your Visibility and Explode Your Business"*

"Reading Steve Kayser's *The Greatest Words You've Never Heard* I was reminded again that Steve's writing has the power to touch, entertain and inspire."

Charlie Bowyer, Executive Creative Director, ABC Entertainment

"Steve Kayser has delivered one of the most profoundly motivational books I've seen in years! These stories will help you succeed in business, raise your kids, be a better person and friend and leave a legacy. They are playful, painful and gloriously revealing of human nature and our yearning to matter. The uncovered gems are found in potent stories, profound recognitions and astonishing poetry. They are words that need to be heard!"

Dr. Rick Kirschner, coauthor of the international bestseller, *Dealing with People You Can't Stand: How to Bring Out the Best in People at Their Worst,* and *How to Click with People: The Secret to Better Relationships*

"This book is a MUST READ! Steve Kayser has written one of the most inspirational and motivational books that I have ever read. Steve uses real-life stories to bring to life the importance of being truly engaged in order to improve the world, no matter what season of life you may be in. It is never too late. The stories in his book will inspire you to live a life of *significance* and will give you the wisdom to see that your best years are ahead of you, not behind you. This book will also inspire you to be a better husband, father, friend and leader by simply being a better person

Mark Whitacre, PH.D., COO and Chief Science Officer of Cypress Systems, Inc., also former whistleblower in the historical ADM price-fixing case ("*The Informant*")

"Steven Kayser has created a timeless book filled with wisdom and the kind of short stories that will stay with you long after you read them. Life is complicated and difficult, and it is comforting to have a book like Kayser's to provide a roadmap with many nuggets of insight and plain old horse sense. It is the kind of book that should become a valuable addition to any seeker's library."

Marc J. Seifer, Ph.D., author of, *Wizard: The Life and Times of Nikola Tesla*

"Wow! Thoughtful, insightful, powerful read. Steve Kayser has clearly found the humanity where there appeared to be none, the humor where it was sorely needed and has placed the truth squarely in front of the reader.

Ken Sutherland, award-winning film composer of *Savannah Smiles* and creator of *Lippi, the Musical.*

"Steve Kayser weaves together true stories that are both moving and memorable. If you're at a crossroads and wondering what path to take, read this book for some fresh perspective, inspirational gems, and moments of insight."

Stephanie Palmer, author of *Good in a Room*

"This is a quick but a very inspiring and entertaining read that provided me with plenty to think about, to 'mist' over and, most important, to act on. I expect you'll feel the same. Bravo, Steve. It's relevant, and you're R-E-L-E-V-A-N-T!"

Dave Stein, author of *How Winners Sell*

In "*The Greatest Words You've Never Heard,*" author Steven Kayser may have created the perfect traveling companion. With a read that clocks in at about the same time as your average plane flight, you will find your spirit soaring above the clouds as your soul is sated with words never to be forgotten. These are words that truly deserve to be heard!

Rick Robertson, President, Antic Productions

"In today's fast paced world of instant gratification, it's rare to find a book that you can linger over while you savor each page. Steve shares fascinating stories that allow the greatest of luxuries—the ability to slow down and just think for a while. "

David Meerman Scott, bestselling author of *The New Rules of Marketing and PR* and *Marketing the Moon*.

"When you believe (the third core practice of a positive lifestyle), you understand that the world is about more than you can control, manipulate or influence; that you can redefine your reality and achieve your dreams even in a negative world. Don't take my word for it, though. Devour Steve Kayser's *The Greatest Words You've Never Heard*—every single story of it. Then you will know what you've always longed to know—that there is a lot more to life than you ever imagined."

Dr. Joey Faucette, speaker and bestselling author, *Work Positive in a Negative World*

"Steve Kayser possesses one of the greatest gifts in storytelling – the talent to engage, inspire and examine all of life's possibilities. *"The Greatest Words You've Never Heard"* delves into human intellect, takes us on a journey of the great thinkers and leaders in history, and gives us new understanding and a way to "salute life," as he writes. Kayser shows us that life is a treasured collection of words … to live by and to cherish.

David Henderson, Emmy Award-winning former CBS News Network Correspondent, author, journalist, advisor

"Steve Kayser has written a delightful compendium of penetrating observations about life's miracles. From the life-saving coincidences that saved an entire church choir to the wireless wonders of a man born in 1856, these singular stories will fascinate and inspire you. Read it!"

Martha Lawrence, author of Pisces Rising and coauthor of Trust Works!

"Steve Kayser constantly amazes me with his overarching appreciation of the human condition, so triumphantly manifested in this collection of insights!"

Tim Eaton, Senior Visual Effects Editor, *Twister, Men in Black, Forest Gump*

This book explores the depths of human connection through the words and stories of real people you've probably never heard before. The stories are thought-provoking and insightful; stories of heartbreak and innocence lost. Stories that describe profound human understanding that will move you to tears with words—words carefully chosen whose wonderful and terrible meanings cut to the depths of our souls and lift our spirits. Steven Kayser has woven a wonderful tapestry of words with honest meaning, thoughtfulness and depth of emotion in the stories they relay. This book will be a great addition to anyone's summer reading list, or anyone who seeks to have their faith in humanity restored with true, human stories that matter."

Teri Doty, Editor, *Music Insider Magazine*

"While reading *The Greatest Words You've Never Heard* by Steve Kayser, I realize what grabbed me—a bifurcated soul, part poet and part ethicist, producing copy that sparkles with intelligence and decency. When he tells a tale, listen! You might find yourself being informed and re-formed. It happened to me!"

Dr. Woody Sears, author of *Communicating with Employees* and *Thinking Clearly* —Vilnius, Lithuania

"Stories of success are commonplace; it's the stories of redemption and second chances that are gripping. Because they teach us that not only is it ok to be human, there is great joy and true fulfillment to be found in living a truly human, humane and humanitarian life. Steve's lyrical book is a wonderful reminder of this, and my life is better for having read it."

Shonali Burke, President & CEO, Shonali Burke Consulting

"The Greatest Words You've Never Heard presents words that share meaning across people's lives, change the course of human events, and impart lessons learned. Every story in this powerful compendium will speak to you at some level. Whether you read it cover to cover in one sitting or read a story here and there, you will not want to stop reading and you will want to read them again. "

Charles H. Matthews, Ph.D., Distinguished Teaching Professor, Carl H. Lindner College of Business, University of Cincinnati.

"It's impossible to walk away without being inspired by at least one story in this book. Sometimes when we're down in the dumps, we forget how life is fleeting and to appreciate what we have. The words in this book pack a few punches that will revitalize and motivate you to make the most of the cards you're dealt in life."

Meryl K. Evans, The Content Maven

"After my mother's death, I needed inspiration from outside myself to get through the next hour, the next night. *"The Greatest Words You've Never Heard"* sat on my lap, was carried from room to room, lay on my bed at night when I fell asleep. Nuggets of faith, wisdom, and courage so simply captured, so lyrically written that I could see a path that was once invisible to me. Put this book on your bedside table for the next time a big challenge comes without warning. Steve's gentle soul will touch your heart while it girds your soul."

Dale Wolf, Editor, *The Perfect Customer Experience*

Wow! The stories in *The Greatest Words You've Never Heard* by Steven Kayser are interesting, insightful, heartbreaking and triumphant! '*They Call Her George*' is worth the price of admission as it tells the tale of character building and overcoming adversity.

Brad Thiessen, Partner in Independence Fuel Systems, a Natural Gas Infrastructure company

"Inspirational accounts of accomplishments and encouragement from various walks of life. This book approaches adversity with great determination, faith and hope. It provides great examples for those going through or headed on a similar journey."

Alan Braley, Bearing Precious Seed (the Bible), Director of Operations

"Steven Kayser's "*Greatest Words You've Never Heard*" is a feel-good book with substance. It stands as a reminder of how powerful and moving words can be. As inspiring as it is illuminating, this book is a monument to courage in the face of daily adversity."

Kimela Robertson, Entrepreneur

THE GREATEST WORDS

YOU'VE NEVER HEARD

TRUE STORIES OF TRIUMPH

THE GREATEST WORDS

YOU'VE NEVER HEARD

TRUE STORIES OF TRIUMPH

STEVEN KAYSER

KMP
KAYSER MEDIA PUBLISHING

KAYSER MEDIA PUBLISHING

©2014 Steve Kayser

ISBN-13: 978-1492705529

ISBN-10: 1492705527

Tecumseh image from the painting by Native American artist Hal Sherman, RIP1935–2014.

Cover Design Image "The Rainbow Man" by H. Kopp Delaney (www.Koppdelaney.de)

SPECIAL SALES

The Greatest Words You've Never Heard is available at special quantity discounts when purchased in bulk. Please email sales@Kaysermedia.com for more information.

Humble, grateful and eternal thanks to all who *"butt their heads against the universe"* and win—or die trying.

Part of the proceeds of this book will be donated to the Conductive Learning Center of Greater Cincinnati (http://www.clcgc.org/) for the hope, heart and love they give to children who need it the most.

To Fiona Antonia Maria Kayser

Before, now and forever, my MBPAL

ABOUT THIS BOOK

Each chapter of this book is a self-contained story. So start anywhere … except the end.

The book is produced with larger than normal font and line spacing. Why? It's an experiment. Due to the exploding number of digital and mobile devices, which have over 250 different screen display sizes as of this writing, we wondered if providing additional "white space" and a larger font size would make for a more enjoyable reading experience for all. Let us know what you think?

Editor's disclaimer: It's mainly because the author's eyes aren't what they used to be.

PRESSFIELD & PRESS

Throughout your life, you run across people that positively change your thoughts, perceptions and ideas about business and life. I've been blessed with the great opportunity to interview and collaborate with some of the best writers and business leaders in the world. From each, I've absorbed and learned life lessons.

The two people who have helped and influenced me the most through the years are bestselling author, Steven Pressfield (StevenPressfield.com), who I consider to be the *Ernest Hemingway* of our times, and Skip Press (SkipPress.com).

Steven Pressfield has written or co-written 34 screenplays and is the author of the international bestsellers, *The Legend of Bagger Vance, The Gates of Fire, The Tides of War, The War of Art: Break through the Blocks and Win Your Creative Battles* and many others.

Skip Press is the author of more than 20 books including, *How to Write What You Want and Sell What You Write.* Steven and Skip inspire, but more importantly, they motivate.

This book is the result of a conversation I had with Steven Pressfield. During an interview with Steven, I suggested that he write a book on the story of "Logan's Lament." He replied, *"Write it yourself."* So I did. It's not the whole story; that's for another time. But, it's how this book came to be.

For many years now Skip Press has freely shared his knowledge and assistance with aspiring writers. He is a rough-and-tumble, tell-it-like-it-is Texan living in Hollywood. That should tell you all you need to know about Skip. However, when mentioning this book to Skip a couple of years ago, he said, *"Quit talking. Do it."* A great mentor doesn't just tell you how to do it— they also tell you to get off your butt and *"do the work."*

"When Cicero spoke, the people would say, 'what a clever man Cicero is.' When Demosthenes spoke, the people would say, 'let us march.'"

− Unknown

THE TEST

How would you react if you were faced with insurmountable odds in a life-or-death situation? A sudden tragedy, a disabling injury or the premature death of a spouse or child?

Would you be courageous? Bold? Heroic? Noble? Would you risk your life or lay it down for others?

We all like to think we'd do the right thing. But there's always that nagging doubt, right?

TRUE STORIES

We've all role-played multiple scenarios in our minds where we win the day, reign victorious and save the world. But real life rarely turns out like that. You never truly know how you will react until you're faced with a crisis. That's when the true you will come out; the person who no one knows but you—the real you.

The following are true stories of others throughout time that have faced these difficult questions and defining moments and triumphed—even if they died trying. It's my hope these stories will offer inspiration in times of difficulty and darkness. Let them become your impenetrable breastplate against the challenges of life that we all must face. Or the diamond tip of a spiritual spear you use to fight and win your destiny.

But, most importantly, these are stories from people just like you.

Some are famous, some not. Some of these stories have been cloaked in the mists of time, while others have been lost in the vacuum of anonymity— never told because they were just the tales of ordinary people who butted heads with the universe.

But, there's only one way that these stories can ever be told, and that's with ...

WORDS

They can make you laugh or make you cry, engage or enrage, bring joy or sorrow. Words herald new life or memorialize lives gone by. The right words can inspire great acts of heroism; the wrong ones despicable acts of evil.

Words are magical. They can transport you to other times, places, and worlds.

Words are surely mankind's greatest invention.

But many powerful words have slipped from the pages of history—In fact, some of the greatest.

You know it when you hear these words. They stop you in your tracks and compel you to listen, feel and remember.

Has this ever happened to you?

If not, it's about to.

Included here are some of the greatest tales ever told. Birthed in blood and chaos, turmoil and tragedy, they are symbols of inspiration and hope.

In their place and time, these words resounded throughout the world with all the subtlety of a sonic boom.

How will these words impact you today?

You'll find out at the end of this book.

HINTS FROM HEAVEN?

Sometimes the greatest words you've never heard might be hints from Heaven.

What are they?

Hints, strange events and traces of meta-meaning unspoken; first sensed then connected—like dots. It's similar to deciphering a code or unveiling a message written in invisible ink. Once the message appears, it's followed quickly by an over-arching sense of awe, confusion—and for most—disbelief.

THE SIMPLICITY CONUNDRUM

Messages and *miracles* don't happen these days, right?

I was trying to write a difficult story when I ran into a perplexing problem—a total roadblock. How do you simplify a complex story—one that involves quantum physics, cancer, dying, depression, hope against all odds and the ephemeral topic of *miracles*?

The story was about a terminally ill cancer patient, a licensed clinical neuropsychologist and international bestselling author that you will meet later in this book. He was a doctor—one that believed in miracles as well as the ability to look for, identify and make miracles for yourself and others.

PUZZLING PARADOX

Part of the story delved into the concept of synchronicity—finding meaning in causally unrelated ("acausal") coincidences and events— events that greatly stretch the probabilities of chance and even belief sometimes. The doctor in the story believed that the concept of synchronicity helped him understand and survive his "terminal" disease. The trick, he believed, was to become aware of these events and coincidences in his life and seek meaning in them.

Some synchronistic events create puzzling paradoxes that seem to be beyond our understanding of reality. They conflict with the fundamental principles of our reason, but nonetheless, they happen.

Synchronicity was a term coined by Dr. Carl Jung to describe these types of happenings. During his many years of research and medical practice, he documented multiple cases that could not be explained by mere probabilities of chance. Dr. Jung came to believe that if you pay attention to these events, they could add meaning to your life. They might even help and guide you in a time of personal distress.

All of this was out of my league. Way out. But I was open to at least thinking about the possibility of synchronicity. The problem was how to explain it in clear, simple language and at the same time, incorporate the quantum physics, non-locality and observer participancy elements that were also part of the story, then weave them so that the seams didn't show.

Like I said, way out of my league.

EXAMPLES?

Some coincidences could be interesting little curiosities.

You go to a bookstore looking for a particular book, but can't remember the title. You walk down an aisle and a book falls off of the shelf right in your path.

It's the very book you're looking for—odd, but nothing life-changing.

Perplexing though.

But some synchronistic events can be life-savers, like the following two real-life events.

RATHER ORDINARY REASONS

"All 15 members of a church choir in Beatrice, Nebraska, due at practice at 7:20, were late on the evening of March 1, 1950. The minister, his wife and daughter had one reason (his wife was delayed to iron the daughter's dress), one girl waited to finish a geometry problem, one couldn't start her car, two lingered to hear the end of an especially exciting radio program, one mother and daughter were late because the mother had to call the daughter twice to wake her from a nap and so on. The reasons seemed rather ordinary.

"But there were 10 separate and quite unconnected reasons for the lateness of the 15 persons. It was rather fortunate that none of the 15 arrived on time at 7:20, for at 7:25, the church building was destroyed in an explosion."

- From "Lady Luck: The Theory of Probability," by Warren Weaver

THE ODDS?

What does this mean, if anything? What are the odds of something like this happening?

Is there possibly an undiscovered connection between minds that transcends the known laws of the universe?

Are our minds connected to a "collective unconscious" as Dr. Jung believed? And, if so…

WHAT TO MAKE OF THIS?

One of my all-time favorite books, a classic called *Man's Search for Meaning* written by Dr. Viktor Frankl, described a synchronistic event that changed his life forever. Dr. Frankl had a successful neurology and psychiatry practice in Germany in the late 1930s, but he was Jewish. He knew he had to leave Germany soon or face death. He applied for a visa and after several years, it was approved. But there was a problem.

"I was asked to come to the US consulate to pick up my visa. Then I hesitated: Should I leave my parents behind? I knew what their fate would be: deportation to a concentration camp. Should I say goodbye and leave them to their fate? The visa was exclusively for me."

- *Viktor Frankl, Search for Meaning*

Dr. Frankl remembered thinking then that he'd wished for a *"hint from heaven"* to help him make the decision.

Later that day, he picked up the visa and went to visit his parents to discuss it. When he arrived, he found his father in tears. "The Nazis have burned down the synagogue."

Dr. Frankl noticed a piece of marble on the table. He asked his father about it. It was a fragment his father had saved from the synagogue. It had some scorched writing on it.

ONE ENGRAVED LETTER

There was one letter etched into the marble. It was the beginning of one of the Ten Commandments.

שלך ואמא שלך האבא את כבד

Translation?

"HONOR THY FATHER

AND THY MOTHER."

Dr. Frankl made his decision. He canceled his visa. It changed his life forever. He was sent to the death camps—yes I said "camps." He survived more than one Nazi death camp, and *Man's Search for Meaning* recounts that experience. He wrote the book in nine days. It was published in 1946 and is widely considered to be one of the most influential books of our times.

SILENT SERENDIPITY

Strange—undeniably strange and true. But nothing like that has ever happened to me. Not even a book falling off a shelf to land at my feet.

But maybe I hadn't been looking close enough, because while finalizing the research for the story I was working on I happened across an article that I'd written a couple of years ago. Was stumbling upon this story synchronistic? I don't know but I hadn't thought of this story for many years.

It was also about another terminally ill cancer patient—a woman I knew. I was asked to write a fundraising story about her plight. It had been exceptionally hard to write, but it was one of those rare moments when you feel humbled to be asked to do something that might actually make a difference—if only for a short time.

LIVING WHILE DYING

Trying to complete that story was a challenge for me, too. Remarkably, it was similar to the one I was working on about the doctor. The raw emotions involved, the brutal facts, the stark realities and worse, trying to communicate what it's like to face the everyday issues of living while you're dying—in plain, simple language—without getting lost in data or minutiae that really doesn't matter.

Happening upon this previously written story at exactly that time helped me to remove the block and finish the story.

It made me ask the question that, as I think about it, still makes my head want to explode.

Was happening upon my previous article purposeful or simply an accident?

THE PARADOX?

I struggle with the thought of it being purposeful. It conflicts with my view of reality.

If it wasn't purposeful, then it was an accident. But if it was an accident, it was a synchronistic event that only I could draw meaning from.

Could these *hints from heaven,* or synchronistic events, be the greatest words you will never hear?

I haven't resolved the puzzling paradox yet, but I did run across words from Dr. Richard Feynman that helped me come to terms with it...

"A paradox is not a conflict within reality. It is a conflict between reality and your feeling of what reality should be like."

- Richard Feynman, American physicist

THOSE DEGENERATE AMERICANS

Thomas Jefferson published the *Notes on the State of Virginia* in 1781. In one section, Jefferson addressed some prominent European celebrity writers who were of the opinion that nothing good could ever come out of America.

"They have supposed there is something in the soil, climate and other circumstances of America, which occasions animal nature to degenerate, not excepting the man, native or adopted, physical or moral. This theory, so unfounded and degrading, was called to the bar of fact and reason."

In response to America's critics Jefferson recites a message sent by Mingo Chief John Logan, to Lord Dunmore in 1774. A message so poignant it elicited Jefferson to say:

"I may challenge the whole orations of Demosthenes and Cicero, and of any more eminent orator, if Europe has furnished more eminent, to produce a single passage superior to it."

But first, a little background. John Logan (also known as Tah-gah-ute), was a Native American Indian born in 1725. He was a friend and supporter of the white man (a most unpopular position at the time with other Native Americans).

In 1774, Chief Logan was away from his village on a hunting trip when a marauding band of white settlers treacherously slaughtered his entire family. His pregnant sister was mutilated in what can only be described as a despicably demonic way. Her unborn child was savagely cut from her womb.

Upon his return to the village Logan found the ravaged bodies of every living relative he knew of at the time, from children to grandparents. All of his loved ones—lost. This event, called the "Yellow Creek Massacre," sparked Lord Dunmore's War of 1774, in which an embittered and devastated Logan sought revenge and got it many times over.

But, the Native Americans were eventually defeated in the war, and a party went to Lord Dunmore to seek a peace council. Logan would not attend the council but sent a message that reverberated throughout the world.

This speech, referred to as *Logan's Lament,* was not only memorized by Thomas Jefferson, but taught and memorized by children in American schools for many years afterwards.

It was these words that Jefferson shared with snarky European critics in answer to their superior suppositions that no profound greatness could spring forth from American soil...

LOGAN'S LAMENT

"I appeal to any white man to say, if ever he entered Logan's cabin hungry, and he gave him not meat; if ever he came cold and naked, and he clothed him not.

"During the course of the last long and bloody war, Logan remained idle in his cabin, an advocate for peace.

"Such was my love for the whites that my countrymen pointed as they passed and said, Logan is the friend of the white men.

"I have even thought to live with you but for the injuries of one man. Col. Cresap, the last spring, in cold blood, and unprovoked, murdered all the relations of Logan, not sparing even my women and children.

"There runs not a drop of my blood in the veins of any living creature.

"This has called on me for revenge. I have sought it: I have killed many: I have fully glutted my vengeance.

"For my country, I rejoice at the beams of peace. But do not harbor a thought that mine is the joy of fear. Logan never felt fear. He will not turn on his heel to save his life.

"Who is there to mourn for Logan?

"No one.

"Not one."

The war ended. Logan never really recovered.

Would you?

Mingo Chief, John Logan, drifted into alcoholism and was murdered by an unknown assailant in 1780.

THEY CALLED HER GEORGE

Her name was Georgedda, but everyone who knew her called her *George*. She was a swarthy Sicilian beauty. A powerful 4'10" human dynamo, who bubbled laughter, love and life. It was hard not to like George when you first met her. And, once you got to know her, it was impossible not to love her.

KEEPING THE DARKNESS OUT

The young man she was destined to be stepmother to loved her at first sight. Not because of any intuitive mystical human insight. Not because they really clicked. Not because she was nice. She was. No, it was because she kept the *Darkness* out—she kept out his father.

When George first came on the scene, the young man's father was already twice divorced, with five (maybe six) children (hence the ex-wives), but only one lived with him—the firstborn son of the first wife.

The young man's father was not a nice man. He was abusive and violent—to both women and men. But especially so to women.

Now, with many years of life behind him, the son came to suspect his father suffered from paranoid delusions—but delusions don't normally cause violence.

The heart does. This kind of heart ...

BELTS, BUTTS, BELLIES

When the young man was seven years old, his father took him to a nighttime rally down by the river. It was a festive atmosphere, packed with people. The little boy—whose feet didn't even touch the floorboard of the car they rode in— hopped out in joyful anticipation. It looked like a carnival to him. He followed his father as they made their way through a throng of people. They eventually got near the front of the outdoor stage. All the boy saw as they cut through the crowd were belts, butts and bellies.

Until the crowd parted.

Then, the boy saw a huge bonfire ... and a *burning cross*. Orange flames shot into the night sky, embers snapped, crackled and rained back to the ground. The brilliantly clear night highlighted the flames. They danced like flickering fire demons, belching the smell of burnt wood.

GHOSTS

The young man was scared. He held tightly to his father. But he didn't scream. He was, after all, not a scaredy-cat. He was seven years old. He really wanted to scream. But he didn't.

Until the ghosts came out.

Then he tried to scream but nothing came out—the sound choked off by terror. When the boy finally found his voice his cries of fear could have been heard around the world. He climbed onto his father for protection.

AND SPOOKS

The ghosts wore white hoods and sheets. They chanted a chorus of words, but the only word the son remembers was ... "spooks."

FIGHTS AND POLICE LIGHTS

That made sense to the little boy. Spooks and ghosts were related. He'd watched *Casper the Friendly Ghost* on TV. But for some reason, he didn't think this was the same kind of spook or ghost. The little boy cowered, held tighter and tighter to his father—as any young boy would do when real ghosts and spooks were about.

But, much to his horror, his dad turned out to be one of *them*. A ghost. One who also talked about *spooks*. It was a moment he never forgot. Even at that young age, the little boy knew, sensed and felt that something was horribly wrong with that night. And there was. His father was a card-carrying member of the Ku Klux Klan.

Six years and two violently chaotic marriages later, filled with fights and police lights, the boy's father found George.

HOW DARKNESS ATTRACTS LIGHT

His father was beguilingly handsome, smart and could be kind and big-hearted. That's what George saw in the man she married. But marriage immediately exposed him for the obsessively possessive man he was.

They married. George moved in. Life began to be normal. It was strange. No more ghosts, spooks or scared young man. The *Darkness* was contained.

George had a son named Chuck from a previous marriage. Chuck was three years older than the young man. He moved in with them too. The two young men quickly became blood-brother close. Odd how that happened. It was as if they'd know each other all of their lives. It was a halcyon, idyllic time. Safe, secure, nice. Normal.

But then… it wasn't long before tensions arose. Chuck was a tall, strapping, straightforward young man. He wouldn't tolerate anyone mistreating his mother in any way, physically or mentally.

THE CLASH WITH DARKNESS

By this time his father had returned to his old ways. With George, however, there was no physical violence, just mental and emotional abuse. His father didn't like her going anywhere, with anyone, for any reason, for more than 30 minutes. She had to call before she left, call when she got there, call when she was returning and then call when she got home. If she didn't, she paid dearly for it. All other times, she was restricted to their home.

The son admired Chuck for standing up to his father. It took serious guts. His dad was a hardened Korean War veteran.

His father always packed a gun, sometimes more than one. This was possibly the only true love he ever had—the love of guns.

Chuck eventually lost the clash with *Darkness* and was ordered out of the house. Chuck signed up with the Navy and soon left for overseas. Then it was just George, the son and his father again.

THE LIGHT OF A NEW LIFE

Until George became pregnant.

By the time George was pregnant, the son was 16 years old. She had nourished him, loved him, cared for him, protected him and treated him no differently than her own son. George was the only person he'd seen successfully stand up to his father and *win*—winning being strictly defined as not getting punched in the face, having your teeth knocked out or being rendered unconscious.

George was so happy to be expecting. A luminous light, an uncontainable joy, radiated from her.

The year progressed. By then, the young man was a high school basketball player. It was during a Saturday practice that he received the call.

George needed him, her water had broken. The baby was coming. His father wasn't; he was working and out of touch.

THE BLOOD OF LOVE

The young man raced home to face a scene he was unprepared to handle. George was drenched in sweat, moaning and in severe pain. He got her into the car as quickly as he could and raced to the hospital. Luckily, a policeman pulled him over for speeding, saw the situation and escorted them with lights flashing to the hospital.

There is nothing more frightening to a 16-year-old young man than a mother in serious labor pains— and the thought that he might actually have to deliver a baby in the car. Thankfully, they arrived just in time. George was rushed into the delivery room.

The rest of it seemed a blur to the young man. He had been so self-obsessed with his individuality and coming of age that he hadn't understood the hard miracle of birth. The screaming, bloody, painful event that *love* uses to produce a new life.

YOU READ THE BIBLE?

His dad arrived a couple hours later. The doctor came out to talk to them with a grim and telling look that was easy enough to read.

There was something wrong with the baby.

Seven days later, the baby boy, Carl Henry, died. He'd fought. He clawed to life. But he lost.

Chuck came back home from the Navy for the funeral, crisply dressed, all vestiges of the former brash teenager molded into a fine young man.

As they left the funeral, the two of them driving together and heading for the cemetery, Chuck said something the young man never forgot.

"If you think about it, the baby has experienced something we haven't yet. He was probably welcomed by angels. I read it in the Bible once. Angels always welcome children. Music plays, too. Tell me that isn't cool."

"You read the Bible?"

SEEKING SENSE IN THE SENSELESS

"Don't tell my friends."

"Of course. Never."

After the funeral, Chuck left quickly to get back overseas. The young man watched as Chuck hugged his mother. George collapsed into her son's arms. Just completely let go. Melted.

For the next year, George was sucked into the pit of a hellish despair. She tried to seek sense in a senseless event. But it was an unsolvable puzzle. A maze without end, *meaninglessness* without exit.

There is nothing worse to witness than the sorrow and grief of a parent losing a child. Nothing compares to the agony, and the anguish.

Years later, after laying George herself to rest, the grown stepson found a wrinkled, worn, weathered piece of paper among her personal effects. It described that melancholy, mournful time in George's life.

WOUNDED WORDS NEVER HEARD

It was a mother's wistful and loving tribute—wounded words to a too-soon-gone, seven-day-old son.

Words only discovered after her death by the stepson, a middle-aged father himself by then, who loved her dearly.

These were truly the greatest words he'd never heard.

TINY TOYS AND THINGS

As I look into this room

I see tiny toys and things

I hear little laughs and cries

And the silence a lullaby brings

All through the night I am aware

Of noises of all kinds

That could arouse and scare

This little child of mine

As I leave this room alone

And go on life's way

I realize it was all I ever wanted

My baby came ... but he couldn't stay

IF ONLY IT HAD ENDED THERE

It was August 1975. The son spoke to Chuck via a ship-to-shore phone hookup a month before Chuck's 21st birthday. The news was not only cool, but wonderful. Chuck was coming home; his enlistment was nearly over, his service successfully rendered to the country. He'd grown and matured in a way that only the military can effect. Chuck was ready to start his adult life and make his dent in the universe. The bonding of brothers doesn't always include blood. They were not brothers by blood, but they were brothers in the truest sense of the word.

Two days later, a dark blue car showed up in their driveway—U.S. Navy. Two officers came to the door. Most of the conversation was shushed by a roaring wind in his ears, a howling silence of agony, if that makes any sense. But the son did hear this: "There is no easy way to tell you this; your son has died."

STOP HERE

It took a month to get Chuck's body back to America.

George had lost her only two biological children in a little over a year.

There are no words to describe her sorrow. A black heaviness, a devastating desolation devoured her spirit.

Stop whatever you're doing right now. Think of the two people you love and cherish the most. Find them. Look them in the eye. Hug them. If you lost them both in a year, how would you go on?

ON LIFE'S WAY

Years passed. George went on. Her sorrow, in many ways, nullified and mollified his father's darkness. Stopped it from manifesting as much and in as many destructive ways as it had. But she paid a dear price. Her light dimmed as his darkness began overshadowing it.

IT GOES ON

As the years went by his father became increasingly paranoid. He insisted George never leave his side.

And she didn't.

His father's career faltered, crashed and burned. They lost everything. Then his father had a heart attack. By that time his father saw an enemy around every corner. He had no friends. He didn't speak to anyone, including his son. Especially his son.

No one had his back. Except George.

She was his rock. George sacrificed her life to be his wife. She always tried to shine light on his darkness. Help others see the good in him. The potential. She never gave up on him.

As it always does, life moved on. Thirty years later, the stepson received a call; a raspy, slight, weak voice. It was George. Cancer. Terminal.

LIVING WHILE DYING

The stepson raced to her side. His father begrudgingly let him in—even though they had not spoken or seen each other in over 10 years. George was in bad shape. Bedridden. Colon cancer.

He held George's hand. She'd never weighed over 110 pounds. Now she weighed less than 80. George handed him a new purple floral *onesie* pajama suit that she had ordered online. "Please have me buried in this. I don't want to be cold."

In a short time, the stepson realized his father could not administer George's pain medicine properly. The son carefully explained to his father that George would not live much longer and his father would need help to care for her.

Finally, his father agreed to allow hospice workers in to care for her. They came. They were godsends. Angels on Earth. They eased her pain, her suffering. His father's darkness, once again, was pushed back to the edges.

YOU HAVE TO TELL HER

One of the hospice workers soon pulled the son aside. "She needs to be in a full-care hospice. We can't give her the care she needs here. She's in terrible pain. And … she has lain in her own waste too many times. Your father's not caring for her, and he's probably not capable of it. Georgedda has bed sores."

"Okay, let's do it then."

"We can't. She first has to be told that when we take her to hospice, she won't be coming back. She needs to understand that."

"What's the problem?"

"Your father refuses to tell her. He refuses, and has threatened to throw us all out."

The son pulled his father aside. "We need to do this. Move her. Ease her passing. Help her. Please tell George we're going to take her to hospice— and she won't be coming back home again.

"No, and get the hell out. All of you!"

The hospice people bolted. His father was still scary—even at his advanced age. Plus, he had a gun under every pillow, in every drawer and closet. The hospice people were truly frightened of him.

The son left. Eventually, after several failed attempts to help, he realized there would be no recourse but to have George forcibly removed from the house to the hospice—just so she could die in peace. He called Adult Protective Services. The police were alerted. The hospice workers scheduled George's removal from the house like it was a tactical military operation.

TRUTH, TENDERNESS

The stepson went in with the hospice workers. He stopped to ask his father one more time to tell George she was only being moved to ease her suffering—but that she would not be coming back. Moments like these demand truth, require tenderness and call for clarity. No eloquent orations. No misconceptions. Just meaningful words. At that moment, his father could have held her hand, caressed her face and …

WHISPERED WORDS

"I love you very much. You have so many people who love you—because of who you are, and what you've done in your life.

I'm sorry that things were so difficult for us, but you stuck with me through it all. Only a true love does that.

Thank you for being my wife, my partner, through this life. You saw light in me when others saw only an ugly darkness. We need to stop your pain. Have to take better care of you. We're moving you to a better place. But ... you need to understand this— you won't be coming back."

Those were great words never heard by anyone. His father never spoke them. He didn't say a thing.

The stepson stepped in, held her hands and hugged her. Someone had to tell her.

"George, you have so many people who love you. Never forget that. Ever. But we have to move you to the hospice. The pain you're going through right now can be stopped, soothed. I promise you, it's for the best. On my life. And, soon the boys will be there to welcome you into the light. Chuck and the baby will meet you. It will be a joyous reunion. You'll be able to see and hold them again."

HATRED AT THE HOSPICE

George was delirious and the son wasn't sure if she heard his words. Worse, he wasn't sure if he believed them himself. But who does? It didn't really matter at that point. They were words of a loving hope. And if moments like these demand truth and tenderness, they also require compassion and hope. It just seemed like the right thing to say. The right thing to do.

The son rubbed George's hands and hugged her as they took her out by stretcher to the ambulance.

Hatred is a hard word, especially when you really feel it. The son felt it boil within his heart when they got George to the hospice. It was a hatred matched only by the intensity and violent irresistible pull of a black-hole. Why?

When they moved George off the stretcher onto the hospice bed, a horrible smell erupted. Everyone jumped back in revulsion.

When they removed the sheet around her, the skin over her hip and thigh had rotted away into a putrid, black, gelatinous mess. Part of her leg bone was visible. Clearly visible. The pain must have been excruciating. Hellish.

The horrid smell was putrefaction ... rotted, decaying flesh. The smell was so vile and strong it filled the hallway of the large building.

The hospice nurses and doctors asked the son to leave so they could treat her. When the son came back, George was sleeping peacefully. He held her hand through most of the night.

The next day, one of George's childhood friends met the son at the hospice. They decided to sit with her until she passed—taking shifts so she would never be alone; George would always have someone who loved her present. She earned it. Light deserves love. Love deserves light.

DYING SHOULDN'T BE SO HARD

Early the next morning, the hospice nurses called the son at home.

The son feared the worst. George had passed away without him. He was wrong.

It was worse.

Somehow, someway, *Darkness* had convinced a female acquaintance to drive him to the hospice. He went there to take George back home. The doctor wouldn't let him. He threatened to kill the doctor—and he was packing a pistol.

The police were called. His father was removed from the facility. From that point on, an armed deputy stood guard at the entrance of the hospice to stop *Darkness* from returning.

Living while dying shouldn't be so hard.

HOSPICE HEAVEN

Caring for the dying is a tough business. But the *Hospice of Dayton*, in Ohio, was filled with nurses who made the atmosphere heaven-like. Hospice nurses are incredible human beings. They ease the pain and suffering of the dying—and the living. And they do it with love, compassion and joy. They only meet you when you're leaving this world. To truly love the departing, without really ever having known them, is a road only traveled by angels and saints.

For three days, the hospice nurses eased George's pain, cleansed her disease-racked body, held her hand, sung her sweet prayers, spoke reassuringly to her, never wavered when the family situation became intolerable (the whole *"kill a doctor threat"* was not typical for hospice workers). They never shied away when times were tough. These caretakers were living, breathing, human angels on Earth.

DYING IS A PROCESS

The nurses told the stepson that George couldn't last much longer. Dying is a process. Like life, but in reverse. Her dying process had begun. George's body began shutting down her internal systems.

On the third day, at 2:50 a.m., the stepson was stretched out on an uncomfortable chair, sleeping. Music, like a trickling waterfall, slowly penetrated his sleep. Mellifluous, melodious, muted voices of little children were enmeshed in the trickling, waterfall of music. Boys playing, laughing, shouting and rough-housing. The stepson was confused. He had to be dreaming. Surely he was in that netherworld between sleep and wakefulness. Then …

BRIGHT LIGHTS

A shock of bright light jolted the stepson straight up out of the chair and onto his feet. It would have been an amazing athletic feat if it hadn't been fueled by fear and ignited by fright. The nurse had flipped on the overhead room light and rushed in with a strange look on her face.

The stepson asked, "Did you hear that? Music, little boys …?"

The nurse almost agreed. She nodded her head, but didn't say the words. Her face told a different story, though.

"You hear a lot of strange things in here at night," she said. She turned back to check on George.

"She's passed."

That was it.

George was gone.

It was over.

WELCOMING WHISPERS?

The son reverentially held George's hand softly one last time. A sorrowful wound opened in his heart. It was a wound that bled words he'd wished he'd said. Actions he wished he'd taken, thoughts he wished he'd expressed. But it was too late now. She was gone. He joined them as the nurses took George's body away, staying with her body until they moved it into the morgue.

The son went back to her room to gather his things. He turned out the lights and closed his eyes to offer one more prayer, one more thought of thankful love for having George in his life. For being treated like her own son. For her love and protection. It was then, with eyes closed, he heard the music again. And faint voices, like whispers, but just out of range so they couldn't be heard clearly. That's when it struck him. He got it. His whole body chilled, shivered, but not from cold.

THOSE WHISPERED WORDS

They were whispers of welcome ... from heaven.

It made total sense. What George missed most, loved most, wanted most in her life had been waiting for her—Chuck and the baby.

He couldn't hear the words. They were just out of range. Ethereal echoes. But he could *feel* them. Feel words?

Yes. They felt like joyful wonder.

WHAT DO YOU THINK?

Were those little whispers the greatest words never heard?

Could they have been?

The stepson thought so.

And so do I.

Why?

Because that stepson was me.

SHOUT OUT TO HEAVEN

Georgedda "George" A. Kayser

April 25, 1936–July 28, 2004

William Charles "Chuck" McNabb

September 23, 1954–August 11, 1975

Carl Henry Kayser III

January 19, 1974–January 26, 1974

AN INCONVENIENT GENIUS

The Timeless Legacy of an Untimely Man

How often has one person affected humanity to such a degree that were the fruits of his labor withdrawn immediately from our day-to-day existence, the world as we know it would essentially stop?

This story is about one such real-life person.

Not since Leonardo da Vinci has one person's mind spawned such a plethora of humanity-elevating ideas. You could take away da Vinci, and the world would be lessened by the loss of art, science, brilliance of character and thought, and would go on – but not this person.

For a moment, we'll take this wizard, this real-life person's contributions to humanity away and...

EVERYTHING STOPS

Lights would go off around the world. Trains halt. Planes would fall from the sky. Industries driven by motors silenced.

CELL PHONES?

Dead.

TV?

Dark.

CARS?

Unable to start.

COMPUTERS?

Not without him.

RADIO?

He was the *"Father of Radio."* 'Ahhh,' you say, you know who that is.

MARCONI!

Wrong. But Marconi did use many of his patents, and historically speaking, was a much better businessman. So much so, in fact, that history books wrongly credit Marconi with inventing radio.

WRONG HISTORY RIGHTED

The United States Supreme Court righted that wrong in 1943. But it was too late for this person, this wizardly inventor ... he had just died.

What about fluorescent lights, neon lights, fax machines?

Gone too. He was mucking around with them in the early 1890s.

That's not a typo. The 1890s. This wizard was demonstrating wireless electricity and lights at the World's Fair in 1893.

X-RAYS?

You thought Roentgen right? Not really. Not without this person.

WIRELESS?

Wireless communications, wireless transmission of power? Not without him.

Have you figured out who this person is yet? No? Well you could try the history books. But...

SORRY

He's not there, been removed. And it's been a great disservice to history, truth and humanity. I'll give you another hint. He was on the July 20,1931cover of *Time* magazine.

Still don't know? His other inventions include: robotics, particle-beam weapons, and he was the original inventor of "Star Wars" weapons.

Surely not one person could bring to this earth such a diverse array of inventions over a single life span … let alone history be silent about him? Hard to believe, but true.

BUT WAIT! THERE'S MORE

Remote control, e.g., garage-door opener, remote-control toys, ozone-producing machines, bladeless turbines and pumps, reactive jet dirigible (precursor to Harrier jet), Hovercraft Flivver plane (precursor to Osprey helicopter/aircraft).

CROSSING BOUNDARIES

Surely we have crossed the boundary from science fiction into fantasy, right?

Wrong.

We have crossed the boundary back from the systematic removal of the world's greatest genius from the history books. And believe it or not, it was mainly because he wasn't a good businessman. This man was altruistic – preferring to better humanity's lot by improving living conditions for all human beings.

This inventor created a distribution system that could deliver wireless energy anywhere on the globe. Once his financial backers learned his true intentions, and that there was no way to meter and charge for this energy, they withdrew financial support. This crushed him. It drove him out of town, and in time, history. To that end, he was destroyed, and all have suffered since.

WHO IS THIS WIZARD?

What I mention previously are just some of technologically stunning remains from his contributions. He failed to patent a lot of his ideas, and he wound up simply giving others away – like the telephone speaker.

Who is this person? This wizard? One who counted as friends and confidants such luminaries as Mark Twain, George Westinghouse, John Jacob Astor, Albert Einstein, Thomas Edison, and J.P. Morgan?

NIKOLA TESLA

Did you know that? If you did, you're one of the few.

I asked world renowned Tesla expert Marc Seifer, author of the highly acclaimed book *"Wizard: The Life and Tines of Nikola Tesla,"* about some of Tesla's most notable inventions and the astounding number of Tesla's inventions that have been credited to others.

A HEAVY PRICE

"A number of Tesla's inventions are often wrongly credited to others. Tom Edison may have invented the first workable electric light, but without Tesla's invention of AC electrical transmission, these light bulbs and corresponding lighting systems would have remained highly inefficient.

"The concept of transmitting electricity for lighting and power for long distances is often wrongly credited to Edison and Elihu Thomson of the Thomson Houston company, (later GE), when, in fact, the system was invented by Tesla and moved into the market by George Westinghouse.

"Tesla ended up paying a heavy price to bring his invention of transmitting electricity for long distances to the world."

TRULY EPIC SACRIFICE

"He formed a partnership with George Westinghouse to bring his alternating current (AC) system to the world. Westinghouse agreed to pay Tesla $2.50 per-watt royalties for his patents in order to get his Tesla's AC system to the market. But financial backers refused to pay those royalties and were going to kill the project.

"Tesla knew it would immeasurably and beneficially change the world forever. And, he felt no one else could, or would, do it successfully besides Westinghouse. So Tesla waived his rights to the royalties and assigned the patents to Westinghouse.

"This good faith gesture eventually cost Tesla $billions (with a "B") of dollars. He would have become the richest man on earth at that time. Those same patents also ended up being the basis for electric railway (the subway in New York City)."

EINSTEIN WHO?

Years later when Tesla approached Westinghouse in dire need of money, Westinghouse turned him down. It devastated Tesla.

Marc Seifer went on to say, "the idea of harnessing alternating current efficiently is Tesla's creation, but it is sometimes wrongly attributed to Charles Steinmetz, a mathematician who worked for General Electric.

"Steinmetz wrote two key textbooks on the AC polyphase system but neglected to put Tesla's name in these books. This would be equivalent to writing books on the Theory of Relativity and forgetting to mention the name of Einstein!

"And, as mentioned earlier, the radio is often wrongly attributed to Marconi.

"Marconi was the first inventor to send a Morse-coded signal across the Atlantic."

"This invention, however, is missing most of the key components to what later became the radio. Marconi was using Hertz' spark gap method to create the impulses. To send complex forms of information such as voice, pictures and wireless power, (which led to the radio, TV and cell phone) one needs continuous frequencies. These are actually Tesla currents.

"Tesla's work predates Marconi by about four years and makes very clear that one needs continuous waves, resonant frequencies, transmitting equipment, a ground connection and a receiver.

"When an engineer named Otis Pond, who was working for Tesla mentioned, 'Looks as if Marconi got the jump on you,' regarding Marconi's radio system, Tesla answered,

"Marconi is a good fellow. Let him continue. He is using seventeen of my patents."

WIRELESS IN THE 1800S?

"This is hard to believe but Tesla first exhibited wireless devices at a major conference at Columbia University in May of 1891. Present were many engineers such as Professor Michael Pupin, physics professor at Columbia University; Elihu Thomson, later head of GE; Robert Millikin a later-day Nobel prizewinner for his work on cosmic rays; and Elmer Sperry, the inventor of the gyroscope.

"Tesla actually displayed his *rotating egg* at that time, which explained his rotating magnetic field. This device allowed alternating current to be harnessed efficiently for the first time. The practical implication of this was that this system laid the basis for the great turbines at Niagara Falls – which allowed mankind to harness nature's power for electricity generation."

"Tesla's lecture was such a success, that he repeated it in Philadelphia, St. Louis and the Chicago World's Fair of 1891 (in America) and also at the Royal Societies in London and Paris. At these lectures, Tesla laid out all of the major principles to the radio and even the precursor to such devices as the TV tube and fax machine. Tesla displayed wireless cold lamps, which was the invention of fluorescent and neon lights as well as the principle of selective tuning, that is, how to create separate channels on the radio.

"As a finale, Tesla would send hundreds of thousands of volts through his body to show the world that his AC system was safe. Tesla had experimented and realized that he could generate very high voltages (that is, high frequencies) but keep the amperage (power) very low. The electricity would essentially surround his body and do no harm."

"When sitting on a Tesla coil this way, Tesla could hold up lamps that would illuminate, or he could transmit sparks from metal caps attached to his fingertips.

"Further, Tesla also speculated that the atom may be set up like a solar system. Ernest Rutherford, working with Niels Bohr 10 years later would say the very same thing, and both men got a Nobel Prize for their discovery.

"Bohr spoke at Tesla's 100th birthday, held in 1956 when the Institute Electrotechnical Committee designated the word "tesla" as the measure of magnetic flux density. MRIs are measured in teslas. After 1956, Tesla could stand beside such other great scientists as Ampere (amps), Volta (volts), Hertz and Watt."

WHAT'S THE DIFFERENCE?

What was the biggest difference between Tesla and Thomas Edison? Tesla had a higher goal – helping humanity.

Edison wanted to create products that helped humanity but also make money too.

Tesla considered himself more of a *planter of seeds*. He provided the seeds and let others raise the crops.

PLANTER OF SEEDS

"The scientific man does not aim at an immediate result. He does not expect that his advanced ideas will be readily taken up. His work is like that of the planter — for the future. His duty is to lay the foundation for those who are to come, and point the way. He lives and labors and hopes."

– Nikola Tesla

TESLA'S VISION

Marc Seifer ended our conversation with a view of what could have been and how the world's greatest genius lit the match that sparked his own undoing.

"Tesla had a vision for the wireless transmission of energy using earth's fundamental resonant frequency. He had the ability to transmit great amounts of electrical power by means of wireless. Most wireless systems today send a signal, and then a battery in the receiver (e.g., a cell phone) provides the additional power needed to run the machine.

"But, by knowing the earth's resonant frequency, a sending tower could jump the energy to a receiving tower thousands of miles away. And then from the receiving tower, electrical energy could be distributed locally either by using wires or by wireless means."

THE WIZARD'S END

"But Tesla also had a innate, maybe even naive altruistic streak. He intended to give the world … free electricity. And it was his ultimate undoing," said Marc Seifer.

Tesla's free electricity concept was never taken to market. Why? Money. Financing was pulled when it was discovered that Tesla intended to give the world free electricity and had no intention to invent a meter to charge for it. Financiers aren't in the business of free.

How does this story about the wizardly incandescent lightning-strike of genius, Tesla, end? Sadly. Tesla, the iconic genius, was left out of the history books. He should have been a billionaire, but died essentially penniless on January 7th, 1943, at the age of 87. He was living in room 3327 of the Hotel New Yorker in Manhattan, with a flock of pigeons—whom he considered his only friends.

A SEED FOR YOU

Here's a timely, timeless question for you.

Where does one such as Nikola Tesla fit in our world? Our time?

Unquestionably society would be much further advanced today if philanthropists would have stood behind and supported Nikola Tesla a hundred years ago. Can you imagine having wireless systems since the late 1890's?

Every human being in this world would have benefited if Tesla's seeds had been adequately watered, nurtured, cherished and harvested.

But it's all about money. Business.

Thomas Edison understood this.

He's in the history books.

Marconi understood this.

He's in the history books.

WHAT TO MAKE OF THIS TRAVESTY?

So what do we make of this travesty?

Tesla's treatment and ignominious ignoble end?

For me it's simple. Some of the greatest words never heard by the genius himself...

"Money does not represent such a value as men have placed upon it. All my money has been invested into experiments with which I have made new discoveries enabling mankind to have a little easier life.

"Let the future tell the truth, and evaluate each one according to his work and accomplishments. The present is theirs; the future, for which I have really worked, is mine."

- Nikola Tesla

HERO GOING HOME

"He is one of those uncommon geniuses which spring up occasionally to produce revolutions, and overturn the established order of things. If it were not for the vicinity of the United States, he would, perhaps, be the founder of an empire that would rival in glory Mexico or Peru. No difficulties deter him." – William Henry Harrison in an 1811 letter to the US War Department

To whom was Harrison referring?

TECUMSEH

Harrison was referring to Tekoomsē or Tekumtha, most widely known now as Tecumseh, the great leader of the Shawnee Native American Indians.

At the time, Tecumseh was traveling throughout America trying to rally Indians of all tribes to form an alliance to stop white settlers from invading and taking their land.

Tecumseh's rallying cry?

"Where today are the Pequot? Where are the Narragansett, the Mochican, the Pocanet and other powerful tribes of our people?

"They have vanished before the avarice and oppression of the white man, as snow before the summer sun ... sleep not longer, O Choctaws and Chickasaws ...

"Will not the bones of our dead be plowed up, and their graves turned into plowed fields?"

— Tecumseh, 1811, The Portable North American Indian Reader

Tecumseh amassed a great following, not only for his speaking prowess and bravery in battle, but also because of his ability to challenge and rise above the times.

Tecumseh would not, as was the Indian custom of the time, allow any prisoner to be tortured and burned alive. He shamed senior warriors and elders in one battle with his logic, determination and spirit. He was just 15 years old at the time.

YOU JUDGE THIS DEVIL

Tecumseh soon came to be viewed as a serious military threat. To the U.S. military, he was a barbarous heathen. A red devil. He was publicly proclaimed as a scheming fomenter of revolution. A killer. A murderer.

But history is history, only as written by the winners.

You judge this fomenter of revolution, this devil, this barbarous heathen who left these words behind.

"So live your life that the fear of death can never enter your heart.

Trouble no one about their religion; respect others in their view, and demand that they respect yours.

Love your life, perfect your life, beautify all things in your life. Seek to make your life long and its purpose in the service of your people.

Prepare a noble death song for the day when you go over the great divide.

Always give a word or a sign of salute when meeting or passing a friend, even a stranger, when in a lonely place.

Show respect to all people and grovel to none.

When you arise in the morning, give thanks for the food and for the joy of living. If you see no reason for giving thanks, the fault lies only in yourself.

Abuse no one and no thing, for abuse turns the wise ones to fools and robs the spirit of its vision.

When it comes your time to die, be not like those whose hearts are filled with the fear of death, so that when their time comes they weep and pray for a little more time to live their lives over again in a different way.

Sing your death song and die like a hero going home."

LOOKING FOR A HEART TO FALL INTO

Words.

Just words.

Ethereally whispering through time on willowy, wisping waves of human memories—looking for a heart to fall into.

On October 5, 1813 Tecumseh was killed in the Battle of Thames fighting to save his native land.

This hero was home.

HOW TO STAY RELEVANT IN BUSINESS AND LIFE?

I overheard a couple of acquaintances talking about a person they work with who was "older" and no longer contributing to their business. This person, in their opinion, apparently couldn't or wouldn't learn new skills — or for that matter, even keep up with the skill set needed to perform the job.

AUTODIDACT

Age was mentioned and not favorably. They thought this person should be "put out to pasture." Perhaps this person was too "old" to be open to new ideas or learn new things.

I overheard the conversation because the people were talking in an adjacent room, and I was breaking down equipment from a presentation I had just given. The two people being officious and mean-spirited had attended.

The presentation was about what I considered to be the *most valuable employee* in any company — regardless of education, intelligence or tenure — the *autodidact.*

An autodidact is a person who doesn't have to be spoon-fed instructions on how to do a job.

They take it upon themselves to learn and master not only their required job skills but others that may lead to better ways to do their job, or new discoveries and opportunities for their companies. Autodidacts are powerfully motivated and disciplined people who might not have a college degree but who can "out-expert" an expert just because they have spent hours and hours doing research, reading, reflecting and experimenting in an attempt to know everything they possibly can about the subject of interest.

I finished packing the equipment and left the room. As I turned into the hallway, I ran into the person they'd been talking about. I knew by the mist in his eyes that he had heard them talking about him.

And worse?

He knew that I had heard them too.

THE RELEVANCE MANIFESTO

No one, regardless of age, likes to be talked about negatively by others. But the older one gets, the words such as "too old," "dinosaur," "not pulling his weight" and " needs to be put out to pasture or fired," feel like a poison arrow through the heart. The man smiled at me. But his face couldn't lie. It was a grizzled canvas of worry and insecurity displayed in a multicolored mural of embarrassment, covered with a life-weary resignation. It said, without words, "Maybe my days of being a positive force and contributor to this company — and even to life itself — are over. Maybe my worth is worthless."

We stared at each other. No words were necessary. I hugged him. He shook. I did too. He misted (real men don't cry – we mist). I misted too. Maybe more than he did, but I turned so he wouldn't notice.

THIS CHAPTER IS FOR YOU TOO

This chapter is for my dispirited friend. It's *a How to Stay Relevant* manifesto. And it's not just for him. It's for all the millions of other baby boomers who have already heard or will hear the same thing someday.

The only time you're too old to learn is when you're dead. And even that, in my mind, is open to debate. Learning is a mindset. Life, no matter how you look at it, is a never-ending learning experience.

Here is a test to find whether your mission on Earth is finished: If you're alive, it isn't.

— Richard Bach

You, personally, have to figure out how to stay in a constant learning mode. You have to be willing to learn, unlearn, and relearn in a nonstop churn. No one can do it for you.

LEARN — UNLEARN — RELEARN

The illiterate of the 21st century will not be those who cannot read and write, but those who cannot learn, unlearn and relearn.

— Alvin Toffler

In defense of the person who was slighted and talked about badly, with the supraluminal revolution in technology, social media and new web applications, just keeping up in business—for young or old—is a real challenge. Not easy. In fact, it can be overwhelming. But if you want to keep your job, stay relevant, add value and expand your life's reach, at a minimum, keeping up is a necessity. You have to step outside your life's comfort cocoon.

We know it's easier to learn new things more quickly when you're young. You have a lot of unused and uncorrupted space in your brain when you're young.

THE TIMES WE LIVE IN

Your brain is not clouded with meaningless mental dross that's been drummed into it for years.

But true wisdom, on the other hand, that comes only from experience. It can't be taught, only experienced and then understood. That comes only with hard-earned years of living in the real world.

Now consider this:

- The aging demographics — the number of Americans 55 and older will almost *double* between now and 2030—from 60 million today to 107.6 million.

- American life expectancy is at an all-time high, and mortality rates are at an all-time low.

- The global economic crisis has wiped out, or severely impacted, many middle and senior-aged people's life savings. Working long after retirement age is no longer just a luxury; it may become a necessity.

BUT HOW TO DO IT?

Some people are already feeling the pinch, working two and even three separate jobs to make ends meet. But really, if you live longer, is working longer that big of a deal? Is that so bad? Considering the alternatives? I don't think so. But staying flexible, open to new ideas and relevant to the workforce is a big deal—today and tomorrow.

So how do you stay relevant in your job? And not just relevant—how do you learn, grow, add value to any business or undertaking, and create a life full of meaningful experiences? A legacy to be proud of when you cross the *Great Divide* to return no more?

Based on my observations of people who continually find new ways to be successful, I've made a list of potential ideas to consider.

HOW TO STAY R-E-L-E-V-A-N-T

I've been around many charismatic effervescent folks in their 70s and 80s who are still successful and growing in their personal and business lives. One such friend is 89 years old and recently sold a screenplay for a six-figure sum. Eighty-nine years old and still telling and selling stories!

What follows is more of an ongoing, evolving note to myself, friends and family, but I hope it may prove helpful to you too. Of course, I had to come up with a mnemonic (R-E-L-E-V-A-N-T) to help myself remember these ideas — a little cheesy, I know. But as far as acronyms go, it could be worse.

Let's get started.

This is how you stay relevant in business or life.

RISK

Risk being wrong if it can lead to good. Risk looking dumb, sounding goofy, admitting you don't know something. Risk acknowledging that you may be aging; but with focus and determination, all that means is that you're becoming wiser and more valuable — in business and life.

EXPERIMENT

Become your family, company or business CEO – the *chief experimenting officer.* Experiment. Learn. Fail. Grow. For example, if you're in PR, sales or marketing, you should always be at the front of the learning curve. Experiment. Act purposefully each day to learn something new, to stretch the boundaries of your mind.

Are you on Google+, Pinterest, Twitter, Facebook, Instagram, Tumblr, YouTube or LinkedIn? If not, why?

Do you know what the *Wearable Web* is? No? Find out. It's going to revolutionize the world like Gutenberg's printing press revolutionized the free sharing of knowledge for all people and inspired the quest for liberty and freedom.

How about nanobots? Ever heard of them? No? Why not? Or neural implants to increase your focus, memory and knowledge acquisition? Surely you have heard of these? Right?

We are on the cusp of magically wondrous and transformational times being brought to us by dedicated inventors, entrepreneurs and autodidacts—times where even the definition of being "human" will soon be questioned. Where being endowed with superhuman strength, and intelligence may just become the norm.

And guess what? Age is not going to factor in much.

LISTEN AND LEARN

Think. Listen. Question. Speak. Let those four pursuits occupy 100 percent of your time. If you do this, you'll note that speaking equals only 25 percent of the time.

Discipline yourself. Listen, think and question 75 percent of the time. If you have a big mouth like me, that's a tough one.

Read. Read a book a week. On diverse topics. Not just those you're interested in or are an expert on. I'm doing it myself this year and have found it to be mentally invigorating or soulfully eviscerating.

My first book in this new routine was Oswald Spengler's "Decline of the West," published in 1918. I tracked it down and read it only because it had a huge impact on one of my favorite communicators and quite possibly the greatest mythologist of all time, Joseph Campbell.

Joseph Campbell was fluent in German and studied at the University of Munich. He came across the works of Spengler whose theory was that civilizations rise and fall in cycles.

Much of Spengler's theory, thought and research were later reflected in Campbell's comparative mythology opus *"The Hero with a Thousand Faces."*

I couldn't wait to read it … until I read it.

To be completely fair, it was palatably unpalatable. Like swallowing a dead snake that had been run over 1,325 times and had been lying on a desert highway for days. Difficult but doable. Like eating army food.

I learned something important though. Inspiration and influence are completely and contextually individual. What has extreme value and meaning to one person is completely meaningless or obtuse to another.

Work begins when you don't like what you're doing. Tension, a lack of honesty, and a sense of unreality come from following the wrong force in your life. As an adult, you must rediscover the moving power of your life!

— Joseph Campbell

The *"moving power of your life"* is what resonates with you—and ***only you.***

ENGAGE

Engage. Jump in. Go for it. Do it. Act. Now.

Twenty years from now you will be more disappointed by the things that you didn't do than by the ones you did do. So throw off the bowlines. Sail away from the safe harbor. Catch the trade winds in your sails. Explore. Dream. Discover.

— Mark Twain

Engage.

Reach out to other employees, customers, prospects and new friends via social media, face-to-face or other ways. It's never been easier.

The more human and authentic you are, the more fun and beneficial it will be to all.

And please, really reach out to the new and younger folks in your company or community.

Don't be a dowdy-doubter, whining-whiner or a nattering nabob of negativity. Stretch your mind. Have an honest willingness to listen and learn from *everyone,* even if they are half your age.

Don't worry about conflict either. A doctor friend of mine believes conflict is good. But not "bad" conflict. *Cognitive* conflict. What's that? It's a fancy term for "good conflict." Honest differences of opinion or points of view between earnest people wanting to do their best. When it gets aired out, good things happen. Actually let me rephrase that. *Great things* can happen.

There's only one thing you should never, ever, ever do. And that's nothing.

VALUE

Create value in whatever you do, whenever and wherever you do it. Even if it's value only to yourself. Deliver value to your company, your customers, your friends, your family, and most importantly, yourself.

What is value anyway?

Simple. It's meaning. Something with unique meaning to the people involved. Something they intrinsically value despite the fact that others may scoff or laugh at it. Make meaning and you will make money my friends. But don't only make meaning, experience it. Experience meaning and you will be okay ... even if the Four Horsemen of the Apocalypse are turning into your driveway.

ATTITUDE OF GRATITUDE

I first heard the saying "attitude of gratitude," on an audio book called "The Secret." I'm not sure where the saying comes from, but I much prefer it to "attitude of crapitude."

Life moves fast. People, places, moments in time— all come and go and then disappear quickly behind the misty veil of memory.

And be grateful.

"God gave you a gift of 86,400 seconds today. Have you used one to say "thank you"?

— William A. Ward

How hard is it, really, to take a few seconds out of the day to be grateful?

An attitude of gratitude is not a platitude. It's everything. Your attitude is really all up to you and has been since you were born. This one takes constant reaffirmation. It's tough. Adversity and resistance attack you every day. They will never stop. And nor should you.

<u>NO</u> TO NEGATIVITY

Just say no. No to negativity. It's a cancer. Cut it out. What good ever comes of it ... ever?

Can you think of an example of one good thing that ever came from negativity? Ever?

Say no to negative people. Negative situations. Avoid them. Find a way to attract and bring into your life people who are not only positive but have happy, hopeful and joyous aspirations—you'll know them by their actions.

"From the backstabbing co-worker to the meddling sister-in-law, you are in charge of how you react to the people and events in your life. You can either give negativity power over your life or you can choose happiness instead. Take control and choose to focus on what is important in your life. Those who cannot live fully often become destroyers of life." — Anais Nin

Anais Nin is existentially too existential for me though, so I prefer the George Foreman school of thought. I love George Foreman. He tells it like it is.

That's my gift. I let that negativity roll off me like water off a duck's back. If it's not positive, I didn't hear it. If you can overcome that, fights are easy.

— George Foreman

TIME

Time. It's free, yet priceless. Infinite but there's never enough of it. It's your most valuable asset, but it's in a continual state of depreciation.

Time. Fleetingly fast. Patiently phlegmatic. The coin of life. Once spent, it can never be replenished, nor more earned.

So how can you stay personally relevant in your job now and in the future?

Risk.

Experiment.

Listen & Learn.

Engage.
Value.

Attitude of Gratitude.

No to Negativity.

Time.

But what about the *greatest words you've never heard?* How does it apply to the *"How to Stay Relevant "*Manifesto*?*

The epitome and the essence of the greatest words you've never heard about the *How to Stay Relevant in Business and Life Forever* manifesto come from a self-educated statesman, printer, newspaper editor, diplomat, soldier, tradesman, author, scientist, entrepreneur, businessman, teacher, inventor and philanthropist who lived and breathed the intent and essence of this manifesto several hundred years before it was conceived of.

If you would not be forgotten,

Before you are dead and rotten,

Write something worth reading,

Or do something worth writing.

Lost time is never found again.

— Ben Franklin

MADE IN THE SHADE

Some words are so bold and uttered in such dire circumstances, that when the actions of the speaker fulfill their promise, they are not only memorialized by history but are also viewed as a noble way to bravely live … or die.

In late 480 BC, a coalition of Greek city-states, led by Spartan King, Leonidas, who commanded a force of 7,000 soldiers, faced an invasion led by Persian King, Xerxes, who had amassed a force of between 100,000 to 150,000 soldiers.

Leonidas' strategy was to block the pass at Thermopylae. It was the only road the massive Persian army could use to invade.

After several days of fierce battle, Leonidas' forces were holding the pass. But then a local citizen betrayed the Greeks and showed the invaders a small path that could be used to outflank Leonidas' forces.

Leonidas, realizing he was being outflanked and that his forces would be annihilated, released most of his Greek forces. But, he stayed on with 300 Spartans to fight a rearguard action to allow them to escape to safety.

One of the Spartan soldiers that stayed with King Leonidas was named Dienekes. Herodotus, in his book, *The Histories*, captured the essence of a courageous, undaunted human spirit in the face of overwhelming odds.

"Although extraordinary valor was displayed by the entire corps of Spartans and Thespians, yet bravest of all was declared the Spartan Dienekes."

SHADE ON THE WAY HOME

"Dienekes is said to have proved himself the best man of all, the same who, as they report, uttered this saying before they engaged battle with the Medes: being informed by one of the men of Trachis that when the Barbarians discharged their arrows they obscured the light of the sun by the multitude of the arrows, so great was the number of their host, he was not dismayed by this, but making small account of the number of the Medes, he said that their guest from Trachis brought them very good news, for if the Medes obscured the light of the sun, the battle against them would be in the shade and not in the sun."

Dienekes and his group of 300 valiant warriors fought and lost. These heroes crossed the *Great Divide—in the shade—*on their way home.

SECOND CHANCE AT LIFE

Is there any more captivating, loved or inspirational story than that of someone who works their way up from humble origins to the top of their profession, achieving more than they ever imagined? The monomythic "Horatio Alger"-type story? A true story that lifts the vision of others to what can be accomplished in life—no matter what station in life you come from? No.

EXCEPT ...

... when that same person, through bad choices, bad luck or flawed character comes crashing down. Flames out. Loses everything. Now that's a story that captivates and inspires—in a negative way. For that story, we crave all of the sordid details. How could anyone in their right mind do something like that? Risk everything? Were they nuts? We zero in with smug self-righteousness, confident that it could never happen to us.

Yes, the *crash and burn* story is much more powerful and alluring. We love it more than the first type of story because it exposes the flaws of human nature, other people's flaws that is. We love that scandalous-type story more than anything ...

EXCEPT ...

... when that same person, after having been drug into the pits of a living hell and losing everything, picks themselves up, dusts themselves off, accepts responsibility for their actions and ...

… a miracle happens. They overcome. They start winning again, against almost insurmountable odds.

This is one of those stories. Ugly. Messy. Chockfull of greed, madness and psychosis, but most importantly, also rife with the sublime redemptive beauty of a second chance.

Full disclosure. I know this person. We grew up together. Went to junior high and high school together. Hung out together, found trouble together. I remember when he met his future wife of 30+ years in the eighth grade. We recently reconnected after many years traveling radically different roads in life—at a high school reunion no less. After too many glasses of wine, we both affirmed our love of life's trials and our great hopes for the future.

FROM MAKING A MILLION DOLLARS A YEAR

He was 32 years old, earning $1,000,000 per year and was third in line to take over leadership of a $70 billion company. He flew all over the world in corporate jets, lived overseas and spoke multiple languages. A brilliant scientist, he started a biotechnology division for this company in just 18 months (it should have taken five to seven years) and had it positioned to capture a global marketshare of the product Lysine. Because of his biotech work it was made better, faster and cheaper than any of the competitors at the time.

The world was at his feet.

TO 12 CENTS AN HOUR

Six years later, he was making 12 cents an hour—in prison. Sitting in a barren cell on a steel-frame bed, no mattress or blankets and with nothing on but his boxers—waiting to be shivved. Sliced. Diced. Killed.

WHY?

He was a corporate whistle-blower—an informant for the FBI. Not just any whistle-blower though …

HE WAS "THE INFORMANT"

Dr. Mark Whitacre, aka *The Informant*, as played by Matt Damon in the movie of the same name, came from a little town called Morrow, Ohio. He worked hard to earn an Ivy League Ph.D. in Nutritional Biochemistry from Cornell University and B.S. and Master's degrees from Ohio State University. He also holds two law degrees (J.D. and LL.M.). Nowhere in his worst nightmare did Mark ever think he'd become best known as the highest-level executive in US history of a Fortune 500 company to become a whistle-blower. After blowing the whistle on the company in 1992, Mark worked undercover with the FBI for three years wearing a wire every day in one of the largest price-fixing cases ever known.

UNDERCOVER

The FBI rarely leaves any agent undercover for
more than a year because of the immense
psychological pressures. And those are trained
agents. Mark was never trained. But, his three
years of undercover work revealed approximately
$100 million a month being scammed from
consumers because of price-fixing. Price-fixing
may sound like an innocuous, victim-less crime but
that $100 million a month came out of your, your
parents' or your grandparents' pockets—the poor,
the middle class and just about everyone you
know. It's an insidious crime because it's rarely
detected. What's another two to three dollars on a
$50.00 grocery bill? Nothing. Well actually a little
more than nothing for the senior citizens that are
on a fixed income. It's a lot. And it amounts to
stealing from Grandma and Grandpa.

THE DECISION

Mark and I talked about his decision to be a whistle-blower and how it all came about.

"In all honesty, the reason this case happened is because of my wife, Ginger, and the FBI agents. It had very little to do with me. I was a person who was stuck in the middle of something I had no interest in doing. I was addicted to the money. The lifestyle. In hindsight, I wish that I could have come forward and helped the FBI for all the right reasons. But at the time, I simply could not.

"I became a whistle-blower and an informant because Ginger insisted I come forward and report what I knew. She didn't understand exactly why price-fixing was illegal; she just intuitively knew it was very wrong. In November 1992, almost two decades ago, two hours before FBI agent, Brian Shepard, first visited my home, Ginger forced my hand."

"She decided firmly that she would tell Brian what she knew, even if I couldn't. She was the sole reason I opened up to the FBI that night. Ginger is the real whistle-blower of this case, not I.

"Had I simply learned from her bravery and honesty, the next decade could have been very different. But along the way, I made mistakes—huge ones.

"On March 4, 1998, as I stood before Judge Harold Baker and pled guilty to all counts and waived my rights to a fraud trial, despite any good deed derived from my years as an FBI informant, I could not escape the fact that I had still made some very damaging decisions—again not the actions of a hero. I received a nine-year sentence that day. Many people, including the FBI agents, have said the sentence was way too long. But, the courts decided my fate, and I served my sentence."

MELTDOWN

Being an informant came with a high price for Mark—a complete mental and psychological meltdown.

Mark went to federal prison for eight and a half years for a white-collar crime that occurred during his undercover tenure. He embezzled 9.5 million dollars from Archer Daniels Midland (ADM), his employer at the time. This story has been covered extensively in several books like *Rats in the Grain* by James Lieber, *The Informant* by Kurt Eichenwald, a former *New York Times* reporter and a Discovery Channel documentary called *Undercover.*

But the real story is just coming to light. Prison should have been the end of the Dr. Mark Whitacre saga.

Why?

Because prison ruins marriages and families.

About 90 percent of inmate marriages end in divorce after three years.

But Mark's wife, Ginger, his sweetheart since Junior High, was his *Rock of Gibraltar.* She visited him whenever she could and held the family together in his absence and through many moves.

Prison ruins future job prospects.

As much as we talk about "paying your dues" to society, those dues never really end for most ex-cons. Convicted felons face almost insurmountable odds finding a job upon release or parole, even if you're highly educated like Mark.

This should have been the end of his story. But it wasn't. No, something happened in April 2001 at the Federal Prison Camp in Edgefield, South Carolina that changed everything. At that time, Mark still had five and a half years left to serve on his prison sentence.

A man he'd never met before came to see him—a wise and caring man. Paul A. Willis was CEO and founder of Cypress Systems Research. He had tracked Mark down because of his expertise in Selenium (Cypress specializes in cancer research using Selenium).

When Paul Willis first met Mark in jail, Ginger was at his side, as always. Paul says he knew the very first moment that he met Mark that he was the right man for him—and his company. Mainly because Mark completely accepted responsibility for his actions, had made almost full restitution (which with interest and penalties was $11 million dollars) and had committed himself to a better life of helping people and sharing his story with others so they wouldn't make the same mistakes.

Failure is a much better teacher than success. It engenders humility. Humility engenders introspection. Introspection leads to truth and self-awareness—whether you accept it or not.

Mark and Ginger had plenty of reasons to be angry at the world, but they weren't. They could have been bitter over the betrayal of the judicial system to them and the excessively harsh sentence in comparison to the other defendants. Instead, they accepted it and were looking toward the future.

Paul Willis liked what he saw in Mark, and five and a half years later, exactly 24 hours after Mark Whitacre walked out of prison, Paul Willis hired him into his Executive Management team at Cypress Systems.

Two years later, Mark was promoted to COO (Chief Operating Officer) and President leading cancer research.

Dr. Mark Whitacre now spends his time sharing lessons learned to help others. He is probably the only person the FBI ever sent to jail for almost a decade that actually came back and apologized to them for his behavior.

NATIONAL HERO?

And, as unbelievable as this might sound, he has also spoke at The FBI Academy in Quantico, Virginia about his undercover experiences.

Today, the FBI agents who were involved with Whitacre's case tout him publicly as a "national hero" for his substantial assistance with one of the most important white-collar cases in history.

What does Mark say about that?

"Despite what you may read in various FBI media interviews or see on the Discovery Channel documentary, *Undercover,* make no mistake about it, I am not a hero. Young adults entering the business world need to learn from that. I was involved with criminal activity, and I went to prison for almost a decade.

"No one is above the law, no matter how successful, no matter how wealthy and no matter how educated."

Mark continued, "At one time in my life, and at a very young age, I had the world within easy reach. But poor, unethical decision-making changed my life forever. My hope is to guard others from the same ill fate with my story. It is important to ALWAYS do the right thing."

Four FBI agents along with a former federal prosecutor involved with Mark's case are lobbying for a presidential pardon for Mark.

Whitacre's story is not only an important personal and business-ethics lesson about doing the right thing, it is also a story of hope, family commitment and how to overcome extreme adversity. But more than that, it's a story of redemption and the sublime grace and beauty of a second chance.

But most sublime of all? Mark was able to keep his marriage to Ginger and his family completely intact.

And the greatest words you've never heard?

Sitting in a federal prison five-years deep into a 9-year term, with little or no hope of ever reaching the heights he had once reached, of maybe never being employable again and the possibility of losing his family and even his life, out of the blue a man appears in prison that Mark Whitacre had never met before and says (and more importantly believes) these words…

"Mark, each person has the choice to *get better* or *get bitter*. The difference is the letter "i."

- Paul A. Willis

These words changed Mark Whitacre's life forever.

They can change yours too.

THE WARRIOR POET

He was charmingly offensive. Carefully rash. Callously kind. Prayed on his knees, cussed like a sailor. His men called him *"Old Blood and Guts."*

Old Blood and Guts, AKA General George S. Patton, Jr., is considered to be one of the best fighting generals of all time. His exploits in World War II are the things myths are made of, but did you know *Old Blood and Guts* was a writer, a poet ... and soul of old too?

This complex man, savagely fighting during the murderous madness of World War II, when an individual life was worth less than zero, believed himself to be a warrior of old. Of other times, other places. Many times, many places.

He thought about it. Spoke of it. Wrote about it. But hardly anyone remembers ... these words are lost to another time, another place.

His poem, *Through a Glass Darkly*, is an amazing testament to the timeless warrior. Each time I read it, I marvel at the intellectual magnificence of this sagacious warrior.

One who sinned and suffered. Played hero and knave. Lived life under fire—from battle and politics. One who overcame innumerable obstacles of time, place and his own irascible personality.

He was a man who took the time and listened to another older, wiser voice—an inner voice—and then battled forward.

THROUGH A GLASS DARKLY

By General George S. Patton, Jr.

Through the travail of the ages,

Midst the pomp and toil of war,

Have I fought and strove and perished

Countless times upon this star

In the form of many people

In all panoplies of time

Have I seen the luring vision

Of the Victory Maid, sublime.

I have battled for fresh mammoth,

I have warred for pastures new,

I have listed to the whispers

When the race trek instinct grew.

I have known the call to battle

In each changeless changing shape

From the high souled voice of conscience

To the beastly lust for rape.

I have sinned and I have suffered,

Played the hero and the knave;

Fought for belly, shame, or country,

And for each have found a grave.

I cannot name my battles

For the visions are not clear,

Yet, I see the twisted faces

And I feel the rending spear.

Perhaps I stabbed our Savior

In His sacred helpless side.

Yet, I've called His name in blessing

When after times I died.

In the dimness of the shadows

Where we hairy heathens warred,

I can taste in thought the lifeblood;

We used teeth before the sword.

While in later clearer vision

I can sense the coppery sweat,

Feel the pikes grow wet and slippery

When our Phalanx, Cyrus met.

Hear the rattle of the harness

Where the Persian darts bounced clear,

See their chariots wheel in panic

From the Hoplite's leveled spear.

See the goal grow monthly longer,

Reaching for the walls of Tyre.

Hear the crash of tons of granite,

Smell the quenchless eastern fire.

Still more clearly as a Roman,

Can I see the Legion close,

As our third rank moved in forward

And the short sword found our foes.

Once again I feel the anguish

Of that blistering treeless plain

When the Parthian showered death bolts,

And our discipline was in vain.

I remember all the suffering

Of those arrows in my neck.

et, I stabbed a grinning savage

As I died upon my back.

Once again I smell the heat sparks

When my Flemish plate gave way

And the lance ripped through my entrails

As on Crecy's field I lay.

In the windless, blinding stillness

Of the glittering tropic sea

I can see the bubbles rising

Where we set the captives free.

Midst the spume of half a tempest

I have heard the bulwarks go

When the crashing, point blank round shot

Sent destruction to our foe.

I have fought with gun and cutlass

On the red and slippery deck

With all Hell aflame within me

And a rope around my neck.

And still later as a General

Have I galloped with Murat

When we laughed at death and numbers

Trusting in the Emperor's Star.

Till at last our star faded,

And we shouted to our doom

Where the sunken road of Ohein

Closed us in its quivering gloom.

So but now with Tanks a'clatter

Have I waddled on the foe

Belching death at twenty paces,

By the star shell's ghastly glow.

So as through a glass, and darkly

The age long strife I see

Where I fought in many guises,

Many names, but always me.

And I see not in my blindness

What the objects were I wrought,

But as God rules o'er our bickerings

It was through His will I fought.

So forever in the future,

Shall I battle as of yore,

Dying to be born a fighter,

But to die again, once more.

In December 1945, after helping to vanquish Hitler and the Nazis in the World's Worst War, General Patton broke his neck in a freak car accident near Mannheim, Germany.

George S. Patton Jr., warrior of old, died on December 21, 1945 in Heidelberg. *Old Blood and Guts* (the hero) was home once more.

LOVED AND LOST

At the end of each year, major media outlets run feature stories listing notables and celebrities who have passed away during the year; stories that recount highlights of the person's life.

Sometimes memories connect through space and time linked to your own remembrances of the person. Memories of what you were doing at a certain time and place in your life.

THROUGH DARK RECESSES

Special memories emerge from the dark recesses of time. You feel heaviness, a sense of loss, not only for the "notable person" or "celebrity" that you probably never met, but also for yourself—for the loss of time.

That time. Your time. Your *lifetime*.

Well, here's my feature list. The names are real.

NOT ON THE LIST

This list doesn't have any actors, sports figures, non-reality reality TV show stars, criminals, scumbags, serial killers or people who are famous for nothing except being famous.

ON THE LIST

The entire list is longer than any major media outlets would ever publish.

Look at the names closely. Read them twice. Think about them. Names of people like:

Troy, Coleman, Ben, Joshua, John, Christopher, Susan, Thomas, Stephen, Solomon, Miguel, Christian, Aaron, Armondo, Adam, Stacy, Daniel, Randy, Tavarus, David, Maria, Michael, Janelle,

AND ...

Jordan, Jorge, Brian, Andre, Mark, Chuck, Edgar, Elizabeth, Carletta, Matthew, Ming, Kyle, Pedro, Lui, Jermaine, Ashley, Eric, Kenneth, Steven, Marius, Jason, Alejandro, Jonathon, Benjamin, Isaac, Jeremiah, Anamarie, Luke, Nicholas, Aaron ...

THE LOVED AND LOST

... and on ... and on ... and on.

WHO WERE THEY?

Fathers, mothers, daughters, sons, wives, husbands, cousins, nephews, nieces, friends, lovers all.

NOT BY ACCIDENT

They passed on not by accident, not by bodily deterioration brought on by the mean ravages of time, not because of drug addiction, alcoholism, cancer or criminal activities, but because they had a special job.

A job that ended a too-brief sojourn on this blue-green magical wonder called Earth.

A job they willingly chose. They were…

AMERICAN WARRIORS

Soldiers, finding and fighting their way through life. But then…

A step ahead. A step behind.

A look left, instead of right. Right, instead of left.

Up instead of down. Down instead of up.

A blink of the eye at the wrong time.

And … their life was over.

THEIR UNDIMINISHABLE LIGHT

They were gone. Forever. The flash of a firefly in the night. Eternally courageous spirits riding a *Sonata of Moonlight* on an *Ode to Joy* of living, giving and life.

But … their undiminishable light echoes eternally throughout the music of the spheres like heavenly bagpipes playing *Amazing Grace* … across the *unfathomable unknowable* on the way to their last post.

This list will last forever. It's eternal. It will never be extinguished, only added to.

THE GREATEST WORDS?

How best to memorialize these true heroes?

Laurence Binyon, an English poet and art scholar, did it in 1914. His *"For the Fallen"* is one of the most moving and enduring testaments to the sacrifice of the true *"notables"* of our times that has ever been written.

FOR THE FALLEN

"They shall grow not old, as we that are left grow old.

Age shall not weary them, nor the years condemn.

At the going down of the sun and in the morning ...

We will remember them."

\- Laurence Binyon

Has better ever been said about worse?

So, from this moment forward, whenever a list of *notable people* that have died during the year is published, please take a moment out of your busy life *"For the Fallen."*

AWAKING WONDER

Do you remember wonder? Perhaps you experienced as a child; that time when everything was fresh, exciting, scary and magical?

Wonder, it was like a fire inside your spirit, your heart, your inquisitive mind. Each new experience could spawn breathless awe and astonishment.

WONDER WHERE WONDER WENT?

Then, time goes on. You grow up and get enmeshed in the drama of daily life—relationships, jobs and commitments—and soon the drama becomes routine and monotonous. Wonder fades.

When was the last time you felt the exhilaration of true wonder? Do you remember?

Do you ever wonder where wonder went?

Does it die, or does it simply hide?

I recently ran into an old friend, Rick Crain, from my high-school days. I hadn't seen him for years. He was always one of the good guys; positive and fun. He was also a great athlete with a lion's heart.

We caught up on kids and family and then Rick mentioned that he'd recently attended a high-school class reunion. I had as well.

GLORY DAYS

We both noticed something disconcerting at the reunion. It seemed quite a few people had arrived at a point in time where they thought Life had passed them by.

They went easily backwards to Bruce Springsteen's *"Glory Days,"* but saw no joy in the present; no meaningful path to the future.

They felt no magic anymore. Just biding time and waiting for the Grim Reaper. Wonder had gone. It depressed me. Why? Because I understood it completely. Who among us has not felt beaten down by life from time to time?

As Rick and I parted ways, I started thinking about the *"life has passed me by"* syndrome.

How can one reawaken wonder in one's life again? Seek out the magic? Feel awe? Be astonished again? Is it still possible?

GOLDILOCKS TO THE RESCUE

I crafted a list of ideas that might reawaken wonder. But, I soon realized that to have any real or enduring meaning, the ideas would need to provide answers to two basic questions:

1. Have you considered how every moment of life is precious and fleeting?

2. Do you realize that each breath extending our existence is a miraculous blessing on this blue-green magical orb called Earth?

The answer to those two questions ended up being *Goldilocks* and a firefly in the night.

"Truth is stranger than fiction, but it is because fiction is obliged to stick to possibilities.

Truth isn't."

– Pudd'n Head Wilson

IN THE BEGINNING

It all begins with some basic, unappreciated truths. Start with the ground on which we stand. Look down (unless you're driving). Stable. Solid.

It is the Earth after all.

Now, if I told you that *right now* you were traveling at 1,000 mph, you'd think that I was nuts, and you'd be right. You're not really traveling at 1,000 mph, You're...

SPINNING

... at about 1,000 mph. That's the rotational speed of the Earth. That speed just happens to be not too fast, not too slow, but *just right* for life to exist on Earth—rather Goldilocks like.

If the speed were much faster, severely violent weather and apocalyptic storms would reign—and life wouldn't. If the speed were too much slower, one side of the Earth would be *Hades* hot, the other Antarctica cold.

It's just about right.

What if I added, that right now, wherever you're located, you're …

TILTING

… at 23.5 degrees?

You'd suspect that I was disoriented, discombobulated or mentally distressed. But, in fact, you are tilting; 23.5 degrees is the "obliquity of the ecliptic." That's the scientific term for the tilt of the Earth's axis. If the Earth were tilted much more or less, it would be unstable; it would wobble and eventually tumble, leaving us humans holding on for dear life.

MOVING ON

What if I said that you're not only spinning at 1,000 mph and tilted at 23.5 degrees, you're also traveling through space at … 66,000 MPH.

That's 18 miles per second; 18 miles per second! Boggles the mind doesn't it?

66,000 MPH?

At that 66,000 mph, we have a dancing partner—
an orb called the moon. Our moon is not too big,
not too small, but just the right size to stabilize the
Earth's rotation and keep it from wobbling too
much.

And so, life exists.

In this solar Earth-moon, two-planet boogie, the
"dark side of the moon," which we never see, helps
shield the Earth from comets and meteors.

When was the last time you thought of the *dark
side of the moon*? When you listened to an old Pink
Floyd album?

All of those things are just right.

BUT WAIT! THERE'S MORE

As you're spinning at 1,000 mph, tilted at 23.5
degrees and dancing a 66,000 mph solar two-planet
boogie with the moon, we have a big brother
watching …

JUPITER

Jupiter is the largest planet in our solar system with a diameter that's 10 times larger than Earth and over 300 times the mass. Jupiter's gravitational pull is so great that it's like a mega dark side of the moon. It attracts comets and meteors away from Earth and hurls them out of the solar system.

If Jupiter were much bigger, Earth would be hurled out along with them. If it were much smaller, our Goldilocks Earth would be blasted with comets and meteor boulders from space.

So we're spinning at 1,000 mph, tilted at 23.5 degrees and doing the 66,000 mph solar boogie with the moon as big brother Jupiter watches over, and guess what? None of that would matter if it weren't for the...

SUN

Does it get any better than the sun? Free energy, free light and life-giving heat to ensure oxygen and water?

Would hanging out at the beach even be the same? Any bigger or closer and we'd fry. Any smaller or further away and we'd be lifeless remnants memorialized in icicles.

So, we have Earth spinning at 1,000 mph, tilted at 23.5 degrees and doing the 66,000 mph solar boogie with the moon as big brother Jupiter watches over us and protects while the free energy, light and warmth-giving Sun nourishes life on earth.

None of that would matter if we were off by ...

ONE PART

If the expansion rate of our universe was changed by one part in several trillion, faster or slower, life on Earth would not exist. Our universe is incredibly, miraculously, marvelously just right.

But guess what? None of this would matter either if we were off by…

ONE INCH

If a measuring tape were stretched across the universe and segmented into one-inch increments (billions upon gazillions of inches) representing the force strengths of nature (gravity, electromagnetism, weak and strong nuclear forces), and the tape was moved one inch *in either direction,* life on Earth would not exist.

One inch in either direction, and we would not exist. Not too big, not too small, just right. Really really right.

FINALLY?

Do you know what would happen if the cosmological constant (the energy density of space) was not tuned to one-part in a hundred million billion billion billion billion billion (10 followed by 120 zeroes)?

You wouldn't be here. I wouldn't be here. Life on Earth would not exist.

We live a Goldilocks life and inexplicably sleep in a bed that's just right—Earth.

Each breath we take, each second we live is miraculous, amazing and precious. Each breath extending our existence on this amazing blue-green magical orb called Earth is a blessing.

Now, I tried this string of logic out on a couple of close friends, and they quickly and heartily condemned it as too complicated, too scientific and too far out to be relevant to their daily life experiences.

GOLDILOCKS—TOO COMPLICATED?

Okay, maybe it is for *my* friends. However, I
hoped it might make others at least stop and think
about our existence in this unimaginably complex
universe and how rare and wonderful it truly is.

My friends (experts at highlighting my
shortcomings) also mentioned that I hadn't fully
answered the first question,

*"Have you considered how precious and fleeting
each moment of life is?"*

They had me on that one. I hadn't really nailed it.

I went to sleep that night discomfited and
perplexed.

How could I answer that question for my friends in
a clear, simple way?

LAST WORDS

I woke up in the middle of the night, and to stay true to one of my annoying habits, I turned on the light and grabbed a book to read. That's when I ran across *Issapóómahksika's* last words.

Issapóómahksika (also known as Crowfoot) was a Blackfoot chief and orator that died in 1890.

The words he spoke with his dying breath are some of the greatest words I'd never heard.

Words that were not too big, not too small, but just right.

FIREFLY IN THE NIGHT

A little while and I will be gone from among you. Whither, I cannot tell.

What is life?

It is the flash of a firefly in the night.

It is the breath of a buffalo in the wintertime.

It is the little shadow which runs across the grass and loses itself in the sunset.

- Issapóómahksika, Chief of the Blackfoot Nation

WARM SUMMER SUN

Mark Twain was born Samuel Langhorne Clemens on November 30, 1835. He's known worldwide for his satirical, incisive and humorous writing. But also for his drop-down, rollover funny and authentic, true-to-life character portrayals.

My personal Twain favorite is the lesser-known but illustrious intellectual, *Puddin' Head Wilson,* who noted,

"Few things are harder to put up with than the annoyance of a good example."

Mark Twain knew words like no other. He knew their power, majesty, and the sophisticated eloquence of using just the right word.

"The difference between the almost right word and the right word is really a large matter—it's the difference between the lightning bug and the lightning."

– *Mark Twain's letter to George Bainton, 10/15/1888*

Though famous worldwide, Twain's life was chock full of misery and personal adversity. His business ventures always seemed to go awry.

"I was seldom able to see an opportunity until it had ceased to be one."

– *Mark Twain*

After multiple investments went bad in the 1890s, Twain was forced into bankruptcy. Then it got worse. He went on a worldwide lecture tour to earn money to pay back his debts.

While on this tour, Twain's beloved daughter, Olivia Susan "Susy" Clemens, died at the age of 24 from meningitis.

It destroyed him.

I think I've read everything that Mark Twain ever wrote. Maybe you have, too. But when I came upon the poem that Mark Twain had engraved on Susy's headstone, I knew there was no better, ever … and they weren't even his words.

The words on Susy's headstone are an excerpt (slightly edited by Twain) from an obscure poem called "Annette," written by Robert Richardson and published in 1893.

A FATHER'S LOVE
CARVED IN STONE

Warm summer sun
> *Shine kindly here,*
Warm southern wind
>> *Blow softly here,*
Green sod above
>> *Lie light, lie light,*
Good night, dear heart
>> *Good night, good night.*

Mark Twain understood words. Their greatness. Their ability to express an unendurable sorrow. To reveal a love so timeless it glows with heavenly luminesence.

These were the right words for Susy; the right words for him.

Could any father write better, with less, for a loss so great?

Mark Twain went home to his sweet Susy on April 21, 1910.

BUTTING HEADS WITH THE UNIVERSE

Every once in a while you meet people in life who introduce you to unimaginable riches in ideas, words and ways to live; a person you may have never heard of until one day you stumble upon them. Their acquaintance will change you forever.

This is about one of those people.

MAKING MIRACLES

I was book shopping at a high-end flea market when I ran across a book called *Making Miracles* by Dr. Paul Pearsall. It was in the $2.00 bin, usually out of my economic range, but it looked exceptionally interesting.

So, I saved up for three weeks and bought it.

The fact that it was still there three weeks later was a miracle unto itself. A sign I thought. In the cards, so to speak, and cards are very important to this true story.

This little snippet on the back cover about Dr. Pearsall was intriguing. It said:

"I died three times. I'm back."

Making Miracles was a mixture of physics, spirituality, hope, action and a genuine reverence for all four.

Making Miracles delved into the evidence for a finely-tuned, aware, universal intelligence with some inexplicable quantum quirkiness. It also told Dr. Pearsall's story of dying three times … and surviving.

I decided to contact Dr. Pearsall for an interview. Much to my surprise, (seriously) he agreed.

At the time I conducted the interview with him, Dr. Pearsall was an internationally known author of 18 books, many of them were *New York Times* bestsellers. He was a licensed clinical neuropsychologist and one of the most requested speakers in the world, having delivered over 6,000 keynote speeches.

Dr. Pearsall was also a frequent consultant to national television appearing on *Dateline*, *20/20*, CNN, *The Oprah Winfrey Show*, *The Today Show* and *Good Morning America*.

Dr. Pearsall (Dr. P) not only introduced me to some of the greatest words I've never heard by the most unlikely of people, but also an amazing card trick that will leave you changed forever. It's a trick that will allow you to "butt heads with the universe" and win.

CONSTRUE YOU

Dr. P acquainted me with a 22-year-old woman. She had just begun her adult life and had just started teaching high school English Literature. Then, she was struck down by a drunk driver and was left pentaplegic (unable to move her arms or legs and unable to breathe on her own). She was on a ventilator.

Life for her was over, right?

Wrong.

At that time, the young lady was writing a book about her experiences on a computer that had been specially adapted to allow her to operate the keys with a stick held in her mouth.

A stick held in her mouth. Let me say that one more time. She was operating a computer with a stick held in her mouth.

And what did she say about it?

"You don't have to feel screwed. You can construe. Trust me, that one word has very special power.

"The dictionary says it means to discover and apply meaning, and what a power that is. It means your life is all in your mind. I am actually happier and more productive now than I have ever been. I sure have more friends and, as you can easily see, I am totally free from multitasking."

She still had a sense of humor in the darkest of times.

LISTEN TO THE DEAF MAN'S SYMPHONY

Dr. P also introduced me to Mosha. Her story is important.

Why?

Because in life, overcoming adversity doesn't always mean winning; sometimes it means winning on one's own terms—terms that perhaps only you, yourself, can understand.

BEATINGS WERE HER DAILY BREAD

Mosha was once a dark-haired beauty. But now, a black hollowness surrounded her eyes.

Mosha was death-camp, stick-figure thin. She was death-camp, stick-figure thin because … that's where she was. This was during World War II.

Mosha's face was swollen and bruised. Beatings were her daily bread.

Mosha was a classical piano teacher, and she loved Beethoven. She had been teaching a student *Beethoven's Moonlight Sonata* when they came for her.

They shot and killed her student but kept her alive. One needs classical music such as Beethoven's to uplift the soul and keep spirits soaring when working in a death camp. So they kept her alive.

The Nazi officers asked her to play for them.

Mosha refused.

They asked her again.

Mosha refused again.

Music was not for a death camp, and Beethoven was sacred to her.

So the Nazi guards placed both of Mosha's hands on a rock, and taking turns, they made a game out of gaily breaking her fingers, one by one, with their rifle butts.

Mosha could have played.

She could have given in.

Instead … she defied. Music was sacred to her.

She made her stand, sprawled on the ground in agony. But she didn't give up her sacred gift. She held onto it.

Tighter than to life itself.

And when, through the haze of a misery beyond comprehension, her life finally fleeing for the loving light, she heard Beethoven's music being played in the officer's club, she stirred and hoarsely whispered in her teacher's voice:

"Shush! Be quiet now and listen to the deaf man's symphony. If you listen as he did, you will hear the way to freedom."

– Mosha

DR. P's SECRET

Every day life knocks someone down. A job lost.
House foreclosed on. Life savings destroyed.
Relationships ruined. Love lost. Hope hammered.

Every day someone is beat up by life. Paralyzed in
an accident. Born with a birth defect. Shot by
accident in random drive-by insanities.

Every day.

But there's a secret to help you overcome life tragedies and hurdles. There's a secret to help you turn things around. To help you overcome that feeling of loss and losing, of despair and disappointment.

I learned about this "secret" from Dr. P, and it's *not* from the bestselling book of the same title.

Dr. P barely survived birth and conquered among a litany of other obstacles in his life, total blindness and then finally cancer—*three times*. Dr. P's triumph over terminal cancer and death three times is documented in the bestseller, *Making Miracles*.

NO ESCAPE

Dr. P was told he would certainly die of an extremely rare type of terminal cancer that strikes down young and healthy people in the prime of their lives.

And, for a little extra good cheer, Dr. P was also told that even if his cancer went into remission, he'd die anyway; die from suffocation caused by a deadly virus allowed to attack his lungs by his chemotherapy-and-radiation-weakened immune system.

DOES IT GET MUCH BETTER THAN THAT?

Yes.

He was told the terminal good news on a Good Friday.

GEEZ, IS THAT IT?

Nope.

On that same Good Friday, as he walked slowly down his driveway, the ache of cancer eating away at him, feeling lost and hopeless, he opened his mailbox and noticed an envelope marked *"Urgent. Internal Revenue Service."*

DEATH AND TAXES

Yup, you guessed it. Selected for a random compliance audit of state and federal tax records for three years.

How's that for some good cheer on Good Friday? And how did he react?

He laughed. Laughed so hard he cried.

My kinda guy.

And when I read it, I laughed.

Laughed so hard I cried.

THE SECRET

So … what is the "secret" Dr P taught me?

The "*secret*" was actually a trick—a card trick.

"Life is not a matter of holding good cards, but of playing a poor hand well."

- Robert Louis Stevenson

THE LAST HAND

Like I mentioned earlier, Dr. P had died three times previously and came back.

The fourth time, on July 13, 2007, he didn't.

But man, did he play his cards well.

WORDS

They can make you laugh or make you cry, engage or enrage, bring joy or sorrow. Words herald new life or memorialize lives gone by. The right words can inspire great acts of heroism; the wrong ones despicable acts of evil.

Words are magical. They can transport you to other times, places, and worlds.

Words are surely mankind's greatest invention.

But many powerful words have slipped from the pages of history—In fact, some of the greatest.

WHAT DOES THIS MEAN TO YOU?

A hundred years from now, when green sod lies above, when there is no one left to mourn for you, will something you have said or done be spoken or written in words so eloquent?

Will you have strived, toiled, battled, vanquished and left your life essence cut on the stone of your times?

Will you be remembered like Tecumseh's…

HERO

GOING

HOME?

SPECIAL THANKS TO:

Throughout everyone's life, you run across people that positively change your thoughts, perceptions and ideas about business and life. I've been blessed with the great opportunity to interview and collaborate with some of the best writers and business leaders in the world. Here are a few that I want to especially thank.

Al Ries (www.ries.com), bestselling author of *Positioning: The Battle for Your Mind* and *The Fall of Advertising and the Rise of PR*, for taking pity on a newbie PR person (me) and helping through the years with his brilliant insights and wit.

Marsha Friedman, founder and CEO of EMSI (http://www.emsincorporated.com), a pay-for-performance public relations firm and also the author of *Celebritize Yourself.* Long-time friend, confidant and successful female entrepreneur extraordinaire, Marsha's guidance, help and patience through the years has been invaluable.

Ms. Sam Horn (SamHorn.com), author of *POP! How to Stand Out in Any Crowd* and *Tongue-fu!,* to whom I showed *"How NOT to stand out in any crowd"*! Thanks for your ongoing friendship, support and wonderful advice—good for any writer or entrepreneur.

Marc Seifer (MarcSeifer.com), long-time friend and author of *"Wizard: The Life and Times of Nikola Tesla,"* Marc Seifer has generously shared his time, energy and knowledge as an advocate for Nikola Tesla's rightful place in history. I've had the pleasure to interview and work with Marc many times through the years. His unending passion is to bring the true story of Nikola Tesla to the movie screen- (www.theTeslamovie.com)

David Meerman Scott, the guy who broke the *old rules* and wrote the best-selling *New Rules of Marketing & PR* for his continued advocacy and leadership in marketing and PR. And, for featuring me in a couple of his books proving that even in a B2B environment you can use humor in marketing, declare war on the bane of business writing (corporate gobbledygook) and not be instantly burned at the stake.

Dr. Rick Kirschner (http://artofchange.com), co-author of the international bestseller, *Dealing with People You Can't Stand: How to Bring Out the Best in People at Their Worst,* and *How to Click with People: The Secret to Better Relationships.* Thanks for hanging in there and submitting to several radio interviews with me that included the disembodied voices of Barney the Dinosaur, Rodney Dangerfield and three deceased presidents (provided by Rick Robertson of Antic Productions)—before he got a chance to talk about his latest book. I think I might have bailed if I were him. However, Dr. Rick hung in there—a class act and true humanitarian. If you're as unlikable and unclickable as me, or you want better relationships and a better life, get in touch with Dr. Rick.

Rick Robertson, founder of Antic Productions (www.anticproductions.com), a full-service advertising agency in Dallas, Texas. Rick is the man who can speak in 1,000 different voices. I know, because I've spoken with most of them. Thanks to Rick for doing a superb audio version of this book.

Lt. Col. Rob "Waldo" Waldman (http://www.yourwingman.com/) a true American patriot and friend who is an inspiration to many. Imagine this, being afraid of heights and claustrophobic and choosing to become a combat fighter pilot—that's Waldo. He is also the *Wall Street Journal* and *New York Times* bestselling author of *Never Fly Solo*. Waldo showed me the two different meanings of FEAR: forget everything and run or focus energy and accept responsibility.

Ken Sutherland (Lippimusical.com), creative impresario, composer, artist, pianist and the music behind the film *Savannah Smiles* and the upcoming *Lippi Musical.* Thank you for patiently and gracefully teaching me the ropes of business and art.

Dr. Woody Sears (http://www.drwoodysears.com/), who lives and works in Lithuania, for always lighting a candle.

Nettie Reynolds (www.nettieink.com), long-time friend, writer, publisher and ukulele player, for her support and wit.

Jim Gross, (email: jmblue1@hotmail.com), editor extraordinaire. Jim's always a gem to work with and a professional who sees the gaps and traps in your writing and points them out with a sublime kindness.

Mindy Wells Hoffbauer (http://hoffbauer.us/blog/), editor, proofreader and gifted story troubleshooter.

AFTERWORD

Thanks for taking the time to read these stories. If just one of these touched or moved you, please share it. And, if you have a *"Greatest Words You've Never Heard"* story nomination of your own, I'd love to hear it, please contact me.

- Steven Kayser

NOTES:

1. Logan's Lament from *Notes on the State of Virginia - Thomas Jefferson*

2. Tecumseh image from the beautiful painting by artist Hal Sherman – RIP 1935-2014.

3. Tecumseh *"Hero Going Home"* speech quoted from Lee Sulzman in "Shawnee History."

4. *"Through a Glass Darkly"* via http://en.wikiquote.org/wiki/George_S._Patton#Th rough_A_Glass.2C_Darkly_.281918.29

5. Nikola Tesla's *"An Inconvenient Genius"* facts, research and background courtesy of Marc Seifer.

6. Dr. Paul Pearsall memorial website (http://www.paulpearsall.com)

ABOUT THE AUTHOR

Steve Kayser is an award-winning writer, editor, publisher, former radio host and founder of Kayser Media. Steve has also had the great fortune to interview and/or collaborate with the some of the best minds in the business world (see http://bit.ly/1fHBPP8).

CONTACT:

Email: Steve@Kaysermedia.com

Website: Http://www.stevekayser.com

Blog: http://www.writingriffs.com

Twitter: @SteveKayser

LinkedIn: http://bit.ly/1bYft8n

GooglePlus: http://gplus.to/stevekayser

Made in the USA
Charleston, SC
19 June 2014